California Bar Examination

Performance Tests and Selected Answers

February 2014

THE STATE BAR OF CALIFORNIA
COMMITTEE OF BAR EXAMINERS/OFFICE OF ADMISSIONS

180 Howard Street • San Francisco, CA 94105-1639 • (415) 538-2300
845 S. Figueroa Street • Los Angeles, CA 90017-2515 • (213) 765-1500

PERFORMANCE TESTS AND SELECTED ANSWERS

FEBRUARY 2014

CALIFORNIA BAR EXAMINATION

This publication contains two performance tests from the February 2014 California Bar Examination and two selected answers for each test.

The answers were assigned high grades and were written by applicants who passed the examination after one read. The answers were produced as submitted by the applicant, except that minor corrections in spelling and punctuation were made for ease in reading. They are reproduced here with the consent of the authors.

CONTENTS

I.   Performance Test A: Adams v. Kustom Spas, Inc.

II.   Selected Answers for Performance Test A

III.   Performance Test B: Rock v. Davis

IV.   Selected Answers for Performance Test B

February 2014

California
Bar
Examination

Performance Test A
INSTRUCTIONS AND FILE

ADAMS v. KUSTOM SPAS, INC.

Instructions...

FILE

Memorandum to Applicant from William C. Baines....................................

Memorandum Regarding Persuasive Briefs...

Excerpts from Transcript of Arbitration Hearing.......................................

Seller/Broker Agreement – Nonexclusive **[Exhibit A]**...............................

Letter from Brianna Adams to Columbia Title Company **[Exhibit B]**............

Seller/Broker Agreement – Exclusive **[Exhibit C]**....................................

Letter from Charles Smith to Columbia Title Company **[Exhibit D]**..............

ADAMS v. KUSTOM SPAS, INC.

INSTRUCTIONS

1.   This performance test is designed to evaluate your ability to handle a select number of legal authorities in the context of a factual problem involving a client.

2.   The problem is set in the fictional State of Columbia, one of the United States.

3.   You will have two sets of materials with which to work: a File and a Library.

4.   The File contains factual materials about your case. The first document is a memorandum containing the instructions for the tasks you are to complete.

5.   The Library contains the legal authorities needed to complete the tasks. The case reports may be real, modified, or written solely for the purpose of this performance test. If the cases appear familiar to you, do not assume that they are precisely the same as you have read before. Read each thoroughly, as if it were new to you. You should assume that cases were decided in the jurisdictions and on the dates shown. In citing cases from the Library, you may use abbreviations and omit page citations.

6.   You should concentrate on the materials provided, but you should also bring to bear on the problem your general knowledge of the law. What you have learned in law school and elsewhere provides the general background for analyzing the problem; the File and Library provide the specific materials with which you must work.

7.   Although there are no restrictions on how you apportion your time, you should probably allocate at least 90 minutes to reading and organizing before you begin preparing your response.

8.   Your response will be graded on its compliance with instructions and on its content, thoroughness, and organization.

MALLIN, BAINES & ARTHUR
ATTORNEYS AT LAW
Midvale, Columbia

MEMORANDUM

TO: Applicant

FROM: William C. Baines

DATE: February 25, 2014

SUBJECT: Brianna Adams & Associates v. Kustom Spas, Inc.

Our client, Brianna Adams, is a licensed broker who specializes in finding buyers for small businesses for sale in Columbia. Ms. Adams entered into a six-month listing agreement with Kustom Spas, Inc. to find a buyer for the business at a 10% commission. She was unable to put a deal together within the six-month term of the agreement, but several months later she learned that Kustom Spas was sold for $1.75 million to a person whom she had introduced to the transaction and that the broker who had handled the closing of that deal was Charles Smith. Both brokers lodged demands for a commission on the sale with the escrow office where the deal was pending. The deal closed, with the escrow agency holding in trust $175,000, just enough to cover Ms. Adams's commission, pending resolution of the contending claims of Adams and Smith.

We have just concluded an arbitration hearing. The issues are: (1) whether a commission is due; (2) who, if anyone, should receive a commission; and, (3) if a commission is due, how much should the commission be.

What I need from you is a draft of a post-hearing arbitration brief that persuades the arbitrator that Ms. Adams is entitled to a commission of $175,000 because she was the procuring cause of the sale, and that her claim is superior to Smith's claim. Please follow the format and guidance specified in the attached office memorandum regarding persuasive briefs. Although you will have to apply the facts in the Argument section of the brief, there is no need for an extensive Statement of Facts. Since we have just finished the hearing, the Arbitrator is quite familiar with the facts, so a fact statement of five or six sentences will suffice.

MALLIN, BAINES & ARTHUR
ATTORNEYS AT LAW
Midvale, Columbia

MEMORANDUM

September 14, 2013

SUBJECT: Persuasive Briefs

Unless otherwise instructed, attorneys shall include in all briefs a Statement of Facts written in such a way as to persuade the tribunal that the facts support our client's position. The Statement of Facts is not an indiscriminate recitation of all the facts in the case. Although the facts must be stated accurately, careful selection of the ones pertinent to the legal arguments and that support our client is not improper.

The Argument section of the brief should contain separate segments, each labeled with carefully crafted headings that summarize the argument in the ensuing segment. Do not write a brief that contains only a single broad heading. Each heading should succinctly state the reasons why the tribunal should adopt the position you are advocating and not merely a bare legal or factual proposition.

The body of each argument should match the relevant facts to the legal authorities and argue persuasively how the facts as applied to those authorities support our client's position. Authority that favors our client should be emphasized, but contrary authority should be addressed in the argument and distinguished or explained. Do not reserve argument for reply or supplemental briefs.

You need not prepare a table of contents, a table of cases, a summary of the argument, or an index. These will be prepared after the draft is approved.

EXCERPTS FROM TRANSCRIPT OF ARBITRATION HEARING

Brianna Adams & Associates and Charles Smith, Claimants

v.

Kustom Spas, Inc.

DIRECT EXAMINATION OF CLAIMANT BRIANNA ADAMS by William C. Baines, attorney for Claimant Brianna Adams:

BAINES: Ms. Adams, please explain to the Arbitrator the nature of your business.

ADAMS: I'm the owner and principal of Brianna Adams and Associates in Midvale, Columbia. I'm a business broker. By that I mean that I represent companies or individuals who want to buy or sell a business, and I put the buyer and seller together and help them work out a satisfactory purchase and sale arrangement.

BAINES: How do you get paid for your services?

ADAMS: Usually it's by commission — a percentage of the price, varying from 5% to 10%, depending on the dollar magnitude of the deal.

BAINES: Which party to the transaction pays the commission — the buyer or the seller?

ADAMS: That depends on which side I'm representing. If my client is the buyer, the buyer usually pays, and vice versa if my client is the seller. In this case, I represented the seller, Kustom Spas, so that's who was supposed to pay me.

BAINES: At what point in the transaction do you get paid?

ADAMS: Ordinarily, it's at the time of the closing of the deal. The usual practice is to open an escrow with a bank or other fiduciary early in the process, and, as contract documents, escrow instructions, stock certificates, money, and other components of the deal are forthcoming, they are deposited in the escrow. And when the parties agree that the deal is ready to close, the escrow holder notifies everyone concerned. At that point, I file a formal written demand for my commission, and I'm paid from the proceeds of the sale.

BAINES: Okay, now, when did you undertake to represent Kustom Spas — that is, to find a buyer for that company?

ADAMS: Back in January 2013, I was in the bar at my country club, and I overheard two members talking about how one had sold his business and retired. The other one, Billy Koster — the owner of Kustom Spas — said he was trying to do the same thing but wasn't sure how to go about disposing of his business. I struck up a conversation with Billy, and one thing led to another.

BAINES: Tell us what happened after that.

ADAMS: Well, I told him that I was in the brokerage business specializing in small businesses and that maybe I could help him. We agreed to meet at his office on the next day — January 22, 2013.

BAINES: What happened then?

ADAMS: We met as planned. I asked a lot of questions, looked at his books of account, got an idea about the history of the business, and that sort of thing. He told me how much he hoped to sell for — $2.5 million cash. After we'd talked for some time, Billy — Mr. Koster — asked me what kind of arrangement I'd need in order to go forward.

BAINES: What did you tell him?

ADAMS: I said we'd need to sign my standard listing contract giving me the exclusive right to market his business for, say, six months or a year. The first thing I'd want to do after that would be to get a formal appraisal of the business. That would give both of us an idea of what the market for a spa manufacturing business would bear and what my commission range would be. He told me to go ahead and get things started.

BAINES: What did you do next?

ADAMS: First, I contacted an independent appraiser I usually work with – Martin Apple – and asked him to do an appraisal of Kustom Spas as soon as he could and to keep it confidential. He looked at comparables in the last year, examined Kustom Spas' books, made some inquiries about the company's market reputation, and came back with an appraisal of $1.75 million, including the company's good will and going-concern value. The company was debt-free except for trade creditors, so it looked like it would be a fairly clean deal without involving banks, lenders, and secured creditors.

BAINES: Why did you tell Mr. Apple to keep his work confidential?

ADAMS: Because, until the deal is made public, you don't want the news to hit the trade journals – to keep the wolves away. I mean keep other brokers from trying to horn in on the deal.

BAINES: Okay. What was the next step?

ADAMS: I met again with Mr. Koster. I knew he was going to be disappointed in the appraisal. It's not uncommon for sellers to overestimate the value of their businesses. Three things happened at this meeting that sent up red flags for me. First, he said he didn't want to give me an exclusive listing; second, he wouldn't agree to a one-year representation period; and third, he wouldn't budge from his $2.5 million price.

BAINES: Did Mr. Koster tell you why he didn't want to give you an exclusive listing or give you a one-year contract?

ADAMS: It was sort of vague – just that he didn't like to be tied down in case some other opportunity came along and that, if I had a one-year contract, he was concerned that I'd drag things out.

BAINES: Did you try to persuade him otherwise on any of those points?

ADAMS: No, not really. I've learned that it's not a good idea to start out the relationship by arguing with the client. Reality about the market and price range usually sets in later when the offers start coming in and negotiations start. So I said, "All right, let's go with a nonexclusive agreement for a six-month period and I'll do my best to market the company at your price."

BAINES: Let me show you a document we've marked in evidence as Exhibit A. Can you tell me what it is?

ADAMS: Yes. It's the listing contract Mr. Koster and I signed on February 1, 2013. It was for a six-month representation period ending July 31, 2013. It's my standard form, and, based on the size of the deal, we agreed to a 10% commission.

BAINES: Did Mr. Koster balk at all at the 10% commission?

ADAMS: Yes. He said he thought it was too high, but I said that is my standard commission for a deal of this size. I told him I might reduce it later if the deal didn't come in as high as he wanted. He grumbled but said okay.

BAINES: I notice that there's nothing in the contract concerning your right to receive a commission after the end of the representation period. Is that customary in the contracts you enter into?

ADAMS: No, I usually include an extension clause. That's a clause that covers the situation where a sale is made to someone I introduced to the deal after my contract is up. This time, however, I decided not to.

BAINES: Why is that?

ADAMS: Well, I sensed that Mr. Koster was going to be a hard sell – his asking price was just too high. And he was pretty clear that he didn't want to give me a contract for more than six months. He complained about the 10% commission. I was concerned that an extension clause in the contract might look to him like a back door effort to sneak in a representation period of more than six months. So I just settled for the language in paragraph 4B, which he didn't object to. It left it open-ended and I felt that I'd be in a position to claim a commission if I turned out to be the procuring cause of any sale, even if it happened after my contract expired.

BAINES: All right; how did you go about generating interest in buyers for Kustom Spas?

ADAMS: I advertised in the trade journals, you know, an ad describing the opportunity and stating, "See Brianna Adams and Associates for details." I contacted people I knew from prior deals who had expressed interest in buying a business. I also followed some leads Mr. Koster gave me – acquaintances of his who he said were hot prospects.

BAINES: Did your efforts generate any interest?

ADAMS: At first, beginning about the middle of February, there was the usual flurry of activity with maybe a dozen inquiries, but nothing very serious. The only one that seemed to hold any promise was from Artie Baylor, owner of Midvale Pool and Spa Service. In late April, a broker representing Mr. Baylor came to me and said that Mr. Baylor had been thinking about getting into the manufacturing end of the business and might be interested if the price was right. It was a fairly serious inquiry, and I really thought it was going to produce a deal.

BAINES: You said that, when you met with Mr. Koster, he gave you some leads of possible buyers. Was Mr. Baylor one of those leads?

ADAMS: No. As far as I know, Mr. Baylor and his broker responded to one of the ads I had placed in the trade journals.

BAINES: What happened next?

ADAMS: Well, I gave Mr. Baylor's broker the details about the company and the $2.5 million asking price, I introduced him to Mr. Koster, negotiated a confidentiality agreement, and made arrangements for Mr. Baylor's accountants to examine the company's books. A few weeks later, Mr. Baylor's broker came back to me with an appraisal he obtained – that appraisal valued the business at $1.5 million. That was lower than my appraisal of $1.75 million.

BAINES: Did you keep Mr. Koster informed of what was going on?

ADAMS: Oh yes, every step of the way. We had frequent telephone conversations. I told him I was continuing to solicit offers but that, so far, the only credible prospect was from Midvale Pool and Spa. I told him about Baylor's $1.5 million appraisal, but that I was confident I could get him off that figure. So, Mr. Koster told me to keep negotiating — but he reminded me of his $2.5 million asking price and that he wasn't going to drop very much off that number, especially since my commission was so high.

BAINES: What did you do after that?

ADAMS: I got into some very intense negotiations with Mr. Baylor and his broker. I argued that my appraisal was more realistic than theirs, that their appraisal had not taken good will into account. I told them that, even if there was a bit of a premium in the $1.75 million appraisal, it was worth it to Mr. Baylor because Kustom Spas was a going concern, and he could capitalize on his existing connections in the spa industry.

BAINES: Did you make any headway?

ADAMS: Not at first. We kept talking intermittently through about mid-June. Mr. Baylor said he wasn't unalterably opposed to making an offer of $1.75 million, but the real problem was that he just couldn't get the bank financing to swing such a deal. I told him and his broker that I had some financing sources and that I might be able to help solve that problem. They told me to go ahead and see what I could do.

BAINES: Were you able to do anything?

ADAMS: Yes, I arranged for a loan broker I worked with a lot – Vinny Maniscalco Loan Company and Forcible Collection Agency – to commit to making Baylor a loan on fairly favorable terms. With that loan commitment in hand, Mr. Baylor agreed to make an offer of $1.75 million.

BAINES: Did you think there was any chance that Mr. Koster would accept such an offer?

ADAMS: Yeah, I thought there was a chance. I had kept him informed all along and told him that Baylor was the only serious prospect we had and that I didn't think he was going to meet the asking price.

BAINES: What did he say to that?

ADAMS: He was noncommittal. He said to bring him the best offer I could get and he'd consider it.

BAINES: What did you do next?

ADAMS: I helped Baylor's broker write up the offer at $1.75 million cash. I worked with Mr. Koster's attorney to draft some transfer documents, and then I took the whole package to Mr. Koster. Also, I opened an escrow at Columbia Title Company. That was about the end of June.

BAINES: What next?

ADAMS: I took the offer to Mr. Koster, and we discussed it at length. He said he wasn't happy with it and, if that was the best I could do, he was disappointed. I tried to convince him that the appraisal I had obtained was reliable and was probably the best he was going to be able to do. He told me that he was firm on his $2.5 million price and to go negotiate some more.

BAINES: Did you?

ADAMS: Yes, but I didn't get anywhere. Baylor just couldn't get the financing. It looked pretty much like a dead end, and no other prospects had developed. From that point on, I kept trying to call Mr. Koster – maybe six or seven times – to see if he'd had any second thoughts, but he wouldn't return my phone calls. July 31st came and went and my contract ran out.

BAINES: Is that your last contact with the transaction?

ADAMS: For a while it was. Then, in early November 2013, I heard through the grapevine that there was a deal pending between Kustom Spas and Midvale Pool and Spa Service. I called Mr. Baylor's broker, but he wouldn't tell me anything other than that Baylor had ended up contracting to buy the company and that he would receive his commission from Mr. Baylor. I found out that Columbia Title Company still had an escrow pending and filed a written demand for my 10% commission. In fact, I was surprised to learn that the escrow number was the same one I had opened back in June 2013.

BAINES: Let me show you a document we've marked as Exhibit B. Can you tell me what that is?

ADAMS: Yes. That's the demand I filed with Columbia Title Company for my commission.

BAINES: Tell us what more you heard about how the deal had gone down.

Objection by ANDREW WELLS, attorney for Claimant, Charles Smith: Objection, Ms. Arbitrator. That calls for hearsay.

ARBITRATOR: That's correct. Mr. Baines, how do you respond?

BAINES: I'll withdraw the question for now, Ms. Arbitrator. I believe we can get in the evidence we need through Charles Smith and William Koster, who are going to be called as witnesses. No further questions of Ms. Adams.

ARBITRATOR: Mr. Wells, do you wish to cross-examine Ms. Adams?

WELLS: Just a few questions, Ms. Arbitrator.

CROSS-EXAMINATION OF CLAIMANT BRIANNA ADAMS by Andrew Wells, attorney for Claimant Charles Smith:

WELLS: Ms. Adams, you testified that Mr. Koster declined to give you a contract term of more than six months — from February 1 to July 31, 2013. Is that right?

ADAMS: Yes, that's right.

WELLS: So, that must mean that you expected and understood that your representation of Kustom Spas completely ended on July 31st. Correct?

ADAMS: Yes.

WELLS: And that, after that date, you no longer had the contractual or agency power to deal with anyone regarding the sale of Kustom Spas?

ADAMS: I guess that's correct, but there was certainly nothing to stop me from following up or referring potential buyers to Mr. Koster after July 31st.

WELLS: Well, as a matter of fact, you never did refer anyone to him after July 31st, did you?

ADAMS: Not exactly, but he ended up selling to Mr. Baylor. I had worked up the deal and referred Mr. Baylor to Mr. Koster during my representation period.

WELLS: But it's true, isn't it, that you completely lost contact with the transaction and had absolutely nothing to do with referring Mr. Baylor after July 31st ?

ADAMS: That's right, but so what?

WELLS: No further questions.

DIRECT EXAMINATION OF CLAIMANT CHARLES SMITH by Andrew Wells, attorney for Claimant Charles Smith:

WELLS: Mr. Smith, will you please explain to the Arbitrator how you became involved in the purchase and sale transaction between Midvale Pool and Spa and Kustom Spas?

SMITH: Yes. I'm old friends with Artie Baylor, the owner of Midvale Pool and Spa. Back in September 2013, we met for lunch one day, and Artie started telling me about how he had tried to buy Kustom Spas but that he couldn't meet Mr. Koster's price. He said he'd still like to buy the company but that his own broker didn't hold out much hope. Anyway, I said that I knew Billy Koster and maybe I could talk to him.

WELLS: Are you a broker?

SMITH: Well, not in the business brokerage end of things. I'm actually a licensed real estate broker, but I've done business deals before.

WELLS: Did you make any effort to contact Mr. Koster?

SMITH: Yes. I had heard that Mr. Koster's wife had been very ill and that she had died recently. I figured he might be ready to reduce his price and get out of the business. So, on September 3, 2013, I met with him and we talked about that.

WELLS: Did you tell him that you had talked to Mr. Baylor?

SMITH: No, not at first. I told him I was sorry to hear about his wife and asked him about whether he had given any more thought to selling Kustom Spas. He said yes and, now that his wife was gone, he was ready to move on. I said I could probably help him and that I'd be willing to try to market his company.

WELLS: What did he say?

SMITH: He told me he had come pretty close to a deal with Artie Baylor, the owner of Midvale Pool and Spa, but that it had fallen through because of price. Back then, he was asking $2.5 million, but Artie had offered only $1.75 million. He said he wasn't sure if Mr. Baylor was still interested but that he — Mr. Koster — was now ready to drop his price.

WELLS: Did he say what his new price would be?

SMITH: No. He was pretty cagey about it. He said only that he'd drop it by "some."

WELLS: Did you tell Mr. Koster that you had talked to Mr. Baylor?

SMITH: No, not right then. I wanted to get my representation contract signed and sealed so I could be sure of a commission. Mr. Koster agreed to sign a 30-day exclusive representation agreement with me, so I went back to my office, prepared a contract, and faxed it to Mr. Koster for signature.

WELLS: Let me show you a document that's been marked as Exhibit C. Is this your contract with Kustom Spas?

SMITH: Yes. We both signed it. It ran from September 4, 2013 through October 4, 2013. Mr. Koster said the exclusive part of the agreement was okay. My usual commission was 8%, but we negotiated a 5% commission. He said that, since he was reducing his price, he thought 5% was fair. I went along.

WELLS: What happened next?

SMITH: I went back and met with Mr. Baylor and his broker. Mr. Baylor's broker said he still had all the paperwork from the first round of negotiations with Mr. Koster and that he still had a $1.75 million loan commitment from a loan broker named Vinny Maniscalco. He said he was prepared to make the same offer he had before.

WELLS: Did you take an offer from Baylor back to Mr. Koster?

SMITH: Well, sort of. There wasn't much for me to do, so I told Mr. Baylor and his broker to set up a meeting with Mr. Koster and make the offer. Actually, around September 15th, I called Mr. Koster and left a voicemail message for him telling him that Artie Baylor's broker was going to present a $1.75 million offer.

WELLS: Did you do anything else?

SMITH: Yes. I called Columbia Title Company about opening an escrow. The escrow officer I spoke with told me there was already an open escrow.

WELLS: Did you ask who had set up that escrow?

SMITH: No. I assumed that Artie Baylor's broker had done it.

WELLS: Did you stay in contact with the parties?

SMITH: Not really. I just assumed that Mr. Baylor or his broker would keep me in the loop. Besides, I was very busy with other deals.

WELLS: All right. Did there come a time when you learned that a sale had taken place between Midvale Pool and Spa and Kustom Spas?

SMITH: Yes. About October 24th I ran into Artie Baylor, and he told me Mr. Koster had accepted his offer of $1.75 million just the day before, October 23rd, and that they were about to close the deal. He said Mr. Koster had dragged out the negotiations and had told him he didn't want to close until after mid-October.

WELLS: What did you do next?

SMITH: Tried to get hold of Mr. Koster, but he wouldn't return my phone calls and I couldn't find him at his home. I got hold of the escrow officer at Columbia Title Company; found out the escrow number. The escrow officer told me that the escrow instructions didn't say anything about a commission being due me. So, I filed my demand for my 5% commission anyway.

WELLS: Is this document that's been marked as Exhibit D the demand you filed?

SMITH: Yes.

WELLS: No further questions.

ARBITRATOR: Cross-examination, Mr. Baines?

BAINES: Thank you. Yes, Ms. Arbitrator.

CROSS-EXAMINATION OF CLAIMANT CHARLES SMITH by William C. Baines, attorney for Claimant Brianna Adams:

BAINES: Mr. Smith, from the time in September 2013 when you first talked to Mr. Baylor about his continuing interest in buying Kustom Spas to the time in late October 2013 when you learned that he had in fact bought the company, did you do anything, other than the steps you described in your direct examination, to bring the parties together and aid in the consummation of the transaction?

SMITH: No. I've told you everything I did. I was the person who referred Mr. Baylor to Mr. Koster.

BAINES: How many times did you meet with Mr. Koster over the course of your representation of him and his company?

SMITH: Just the one time – September 3rd.

BAINES: And how long did that meeting last?

SMITH: Forty-five minutes to an hour.

BAINES: Did there ever come a time when you learned that my client, Ms. Adams, had represented Mr. Koster and Kustom Spas in an earlier effort to sell the company?

SMITH: Only when I learned that we had both filed demands with Columbia Title Company.

BAINES: In other words, you never asked anyone, correct?

SMITH: That's right. And no one ever told me, either. I mean, I assumed that the only other broker in the picture was Mr. Baylor's broker, and I knew he was being paid by Mr. Baylor. I also assume that Mr. Koster would have told me about Ms. Adams's involvement in the earlier failed deal if he thought it was important.

BAINES: As I understand your direct testimony, the offer that Mr. Baylor made in September or October of 2013 was exactly the same offer he had made back in June 2013 — $1.75 million — using the same documentation and with the same loan commitment he had obtained earlier. Is that right?

SMITH: I guess they had to update the documentation, but, yes, that's the way I understand it.

BAINES: So, your claim for a commission is based on the following facts: number one, you learned from Mr. Baylor that he had earlier tried to buy Kustom Spas; number two, Mr. Koster, without knowing you had talked to Mr. Baylor, told you the same thing and asked you to see if you could renew Mr. Baylor's interest; and number three, you told Mr. Baylor's broker to set up a meeting with Mr. Koster and renew his $1.75 million offer. Is that right?

SMITH: Yes, that's pretty much it. But don't forget -- If it hadn't been for my personal contacts and my reenergizing Mr. Baylor's interest and referring him to Mr. Koster, there would never have been a deal.

BAINES: In fact, Mr. Smith, the deal didn't happened during the period of your contract with Kustom Spas, did it?

SMITH: No, but I don't see what difference that makes. The extension clause in my contract gave me the right to a commission because the buyer turned out to be someone I had referred to Kustom Spas. I'm the one who referred Mr. Baylor, and the sale happened within a couple of weeks after the end of my contract. So, I don't see why there's any question about it.

BAINES: No further questions.

EXAMINATION OF RESPONDENT WILLIAM A. KOSTER by William C. Baines, attorney for Claimant Brianna Adams:

BAINES: Mr. Koster, when did you and Mr. Baylor actually come to an agreement regarding the sale of your business to Midvale Pool and Spa?

KOSTER: On October 23, 2013.

BAINES: When did he first make the offer that you ended up accepting?

KOSTER: Well, I can't be sure. We did a lot of negotiating when his broker first brought me the offer, but it was sometime in the last half of September 2013.

BAINES: And, isn't it correct that the offer he had submitted to you and that you accepted was exactly the offer he had submitted back in June 2013 through Ms. Adams? That is, $1.75 million and based on the same documentation?

KOSTER: Well, we had to update the paperwork, but, yeah, it was pretty much identical.

BAINES: Now, you have refused to authorize the title company to disburse any of the $175,000 the title company is holding in escrow to either one of the claimants – Ms. Adams and Mr. Smith – correct?

KOSTER: Absolutely. Neither one of them did me any good at all. Ms. Adams couldn't produce a buyer at my asking price because she wasn't a very effective negotiator. I should have just fired her, but she saved me the trouble when she just lost interest and let her contract run out. As for Mr. Smith, he didn't do anything other than send me someone I told him about. And, even then, all he did was send me an offer I had already rejected.

BAINES: You never told Mr. Smith that Ms. Adams worked on and presented Mr. Baylor's offer to you, did you?

KOSTER: No, I didn't see why that mattered, and Smith never asked.

BAINES: Regarding Ms. Adams, you knew, didn't you, that she's the one who found Mr. Baylor as an interested buyer, that she had done all the work to put the deal together, and negotiated on your behalf?

KOSTER: Well, I heard her testimony about all the work she says she did to put together the offer, and I have no reason to doubt any of it. All I know is that she didn't make it happen.

BAINES: In the final analysis, however, you ended up selling to a person she had referred to you and done all the work on and for the same price she had gotten for you, right?

KOSTER: Yeah, but no thanks to her. And it was under totally different circumstances. My wife had died in the meantime, so I was more motivated to take a lower price and get out of the business.

BAINES: No further questions.

EXHIBIT A

SELLER/BROKER AGREEMENT – NONEXCLUSIVE

Right to Represent

1. **Nonexclusive Right to Represent:** Kustom Spas, Inc. and William A. Koster ("Seller") grant to Brianna Adams & Associates ("Broker") for the representation period beginning on February 1, 2013 and ending at 11:59 p.m. on July 31, 2013 the nonexclusive irrevocable right to represent Seller in selling all corporate stock, assets and liabilities, including but not limited to land, buildings, equipment, accounts, and good will of the manufacturing business known as Kustom Spas, Inc. located at 1422 E. Industrial Parkway, Midvale, Columbia (hereinafter, "the property").

* * *

4. **Compensation to Broker:** Broker's compensation shall be on the following terms:

    A. **Amount:** Broker shall be entitled to a commission of 10% of the gross sale price of the property.

    B. **Broker Right to Compensation:** Broker shall be entitled to compensation specified in paragraph 4A if Seller enters into a binding agreement to sell the property for the $2.5 million cash asking price or on other terms agreeable to the Seller and the Buyer, if the Buyer of the property is a person or entity secured through the efforts of Broker.

    C. **Payment of Compensation:** Compensation shall be payable upon completion of any transaction described in paragraph B and upon close of the escrow relating to said transaction.

* * *

9. **Dispute Resolution:** Seller and Broker agree that any dispute or claim arising between them and relating to this Agreement shall be resolved by final and binding arbitration pursuant to the Rules of the Columbia Association of Commissioned Brokers.

EXHIBIT B

Brianna Adams & Associates
Small Business Brokers

224 Fremont Place, Suite 129
Midvale, Columbia

November 4, 2013

Columbia Title Company
Attn: Harold Fraser, Escrow Officer
1465 Norden Street
Midvale, Columbia

RE: Escrow No. 421-344B-13
        Midvale Pool and Spa/Kustom Spas

To whom it may concern:

The undersigned, on behalf of Brianna Adams & Associates, files this demand in the above-referenced escrow for a commission of 10% of the gross sale price in the purchase and sale transaction between Midvale Pool and Spa and Kustom Spas. I attach a copy of the Seller/Broker Agreement I entered into for the sale of Kustom Spas and represent to you that I was the procuring cause of the sale to Midvale Pool and Spa.

I hereby notify you that I have authorized my attorneys to file suit against Columbia Title Company if you close the escrow and disburse the proceeds without paying my commission or setting aside the required 10% pending settlement of any dispute.

Very truly yours,

Brianna Adams & Associates

By___*Brianna Adams* _____
Brianna Adams, Owner/Principal

EXHIBIT C

SELLER/BROKER AGREEMENT –EXCLUSIVE

Right to Represent

1. **Exclusive Right to Represent:** Kustom Spas, Inc. and William A. Koster ("Seller") grant to Charles Smith ("Broker") for the representation period beginning on September 4, 2013 and ending at 11:59 p.m. on October 4, 2013 the exclusive irrevocable right to represent Seller in selling Kustom Spas, Inc., including its corporate stock, assets, liabilities, land, buildings, equipment, accounts, and good will. Kustom Spas, Inc. is located at 1422 E. Industrial Parkway, Midvale, Columbia (hereinafter, "the property").

* * *

4. **Compensation to Broker:** Broker's compensation shall be on the following terms:

    A. **Amount:** Broker shall be entitled to a commission of 5% of the gross sale price of the property.

    B. **Broker Right to Compensation:** Broker shall be entitled to compensation specified in paragraph 4A if Seller enters into a binding agreement during the representation period or within 180 days thereafter to sell the property on other terms agreeable to the Seller and the Buyer, if the Buyer of the property is a person or entity referred to Seller by Broker.

    C. **Payment of Compensation:** Compensation shall be payable upon completion of any transaction described in paragraph B and upon close of the escrow relating to said transaction.

* * *

10. **Dispute Resolution:** Seller and Broker agree that any dispute or claim arising between them and relating to this Agreement shall be resolved by final and binding arbitration pursuant to the Rules of the Columbia Association of Brokers.

EXHIBIT D

Charles Smith
Broker/Realtor

42 Empire Place
Midvale, Columbia

October 24, 2013

Columbia Title Company
Attn: Harold Fraser, Escrow Officer
1465 Norden Street
Midvale, Columbia

RE: Escrow No. 421-344B-13
        Midvale Pool and Spa/Kustom Spas

Dear Mr. Fraser:

This is to advise you that I am entitled to a commission of 5% of the gross sale price in the above-referenced transaction. I enclose a copy of my representation contract with Kustom Spas; that contract is the basis of my claim. I hereby demand that you disburse said sum to me upon the close of escrow.

Sincerely,

Charles Smith

February 2014

California
Bar
Examination

Performance Test A
LIBRARY

ADAMS v. KUSTOM SPAS, INC.

LIBRARY

Quincy Sales v. North America Machinery Corp.
Columbia Court of Appeal (2004)...

Ellis Realty, Inc. v. Gable Holdings, LLC
United States Court of Appeals, 15th Circuit (2005).................................

AAA Business Brokers v. Wicks
Columbia Supreme Court (2004)..

**Columbia Association of Commissioned Brokers
Guidelines for Arbitrators in Commission Disputes
Between and Among Brokers**...

QUINCY SALES v. NORTH AMERICA MACHINERY CORP.

Columbia Court of Appeal (2004)

Defendant, North America Machinery Corp. (NAM), appeals the entry of summary judgment in favor of Quincy Sales (Quincy). The case involves a dispute over unpaid post-termination commissions.

NAM manufactures industrial equipment to its customers' specifications. Quincy, an independent sales representative, acts as agent for various manufacturers to sell the manufacturers' products to third parties. In December 1994, NAM, through its vice president Richard Sears, and Quincy, through its owner James Quincy, entered into an oral agency agreement terminable at the will of either party. The parties agree that the only terms of the agency contract concerning payment were that Quincy's standard commission would be 5% and that Quincy would not get paid until NAM got paid. They also agree that, in making their oral agreement, the issue of post-termination commissions never came up.

During the agency relationship, Quincy approached Dorco, a Columbia company, and got Dorco interested in purchasing three machines from NAM. Quincy consulted with NAM, assisted Dorco in drawing up the specifications for the machinery, and negotiated a price and a delivery schedule. Because the machinery required by Dorco was expensive and technologically complicated, NAM was reluctant to commit to three machines at once. NAM's concern was that the machines might not perform as expected by Dorco.

As a result, in June 1998, Quincy negotiated the following arrangement: Dorco would purchase one machine, lease a second one with the option to purchase or return it if it did not perform well, and have the option to purchase a third machine. As an incentive to Dorco to exercise the options to purchase the second and third machines, Quincy offered with NAM's approval to sell those machines at discounted prices. Quincy prepared the necessary purchase, sale, and lease documents, caused Dorco to execute them, and delivered them to NAM. As part of the negotiation, Quincy agreed to reduce his sales commission on all three machines from the customary 5% to 4%. The first two machines were delivered to Dorco during 1999; it paid cash for the first one and commenced making payments on the second machine on which the lease was to run through March 2001. In December 2000, Quincy terminated his agency relationship with NAM, citing "bad blood" between him and certain NAM personnel. In April 2001, Dorco purchased the second machine, thus ending the lease, and, in January 2002, Dorco exercised its option and purchased the third machine. NAM paid Quincy the commissions on the sale of the first machine and on the lease payments through December 2000, which was when Quincy quit, but refused to pay commissions on the lease payments and sales that occurred after that. Quincy filed suit seeking to recover the commissions for the remaining lease payments and for the sales of the second and third machines.

Quincy's theory of recovery rests on the procuring cause rule. The procuring cause rule allows a salesperson, in whatever field of endeavor, to recover commissions on sales made after the termination of the agency relationship if the salesperson procured the sales through his or her activities prior to the termination of the relationship. It is a common law, equitable doctrine designed to protect a salesperson who, although no longer an agent or employee when the sale is made, has done substantially everything necessary to effect the sale. The procuring cause rule does not apply, however, when the contract between the parties specifies whether and when post-termination commissions are earned, which is not the case here.

NAM argues that Quincy cannot avail himself of the procuring cause doctrine because Quincy, not NAM, terminated the agency relationship. NAM's theory is that the procuring cause doctrine is designed to protect salespeople who are discharged by their employers to avoid paying them a commission. We find little support for this proposition either in the authorities or in logic. Once the agent has put in motion the chain of events that lead to a sale and has done everything within his power and authority to bring about that result, it is irrelevant which party terminated the relationship.

NAM next contends that Quincy was not the *efficient* cause of the sale but, rather, that it was NAM's efforts that brought about the sales of the second and third machines. That is, NAM continued to provide services to Dorco after it had bought the first machine and leased the second, and it was through those services and the attention given by NAM, not by Quincy, that Dorco ended up buying the second and third machines.

We do not find that argument persuasive. First, Quincy's job was to sell NAM's machines, not to become engaged in post-sale service. Sears' deposition testimony established clearly that post-sales customer relations and service were the responsibility of NAM, not Quincy. Moreover, Sears could not identify anything that Quincy failed to do to bring about the sale. Also, it must be remembered that Quincy brought to NAM a buyer that was ready, willing, and able to buy three machines at the inception but that it was NAM who, albeit for legitimate reasons, declined to sell the three machines at once. Quincy negotiated the sale-option-lease terms, prepared the documentation to conform to the altered transaction, and caused Dorco to execute all the necessary papers. The structure of the deal, by which Quincy agreed to reduce his commission to 4% on all three machines, clearly contemplated that Quincy would receive commissions on the second and third machines.

Thus, we conclude that Quincy was the procuring cause of the sales to Dorco, and we affirm the lower court's judgment.

ELLIS REALTY, INC. v. GABLE HOLDINGS, LLC

United States Court of Appeals, 15th Circuit (2005)

Ellis Realty (Ellis) agreed to be the exclusive broker for Gable Holdings, LLC (Gable) in trying to lease the Highland Tower Office Building (the Tower), a commercial property owned by Gable in Bay City, Columbia. Their written brokerage agreement provided that Ellis would receive a commission on all leases signed *during* the term of the agreement and that Ellis would receive a commission on all leases signed *after* the termination of the agreement so long as within 90 days of termination "negotiations continue or resume leading to the execution of a lease with any person or entity with whom Ellis negotiated."

Barry Farley, a broker employed by Ellis, served as Gable's primary brokerage agent and, in the fall of 2001, was in negotiations with Firebridge Tire Co. (Firebridge), a potential tenant of the Tower. When Farley left his employment with Ellis in December 2001, Gable terminated its agreement with Ellis. Nine months later, Gable signed a lease with Firebridge, prompting Ellis to demand a commission under the terms of the brokerage contract.

The district court, applying its interpretation of Columbia law in this diversity case, granted summary judgment in favor of Gable, concluding that Columbia common law required Ellis to show that it was the "procuring cause" of the lease and that this tenet of Columbia law trumped any contrary terms in the brokerage contract, including the continuation-of-negotiations-within-90-days-of-termination provision. In our view, Columbia law places no such constraint on the rights of contracting parties to determine whether a commission is or is not due under a brokerage agreement, and, accordingly, we reverse.

On March 29, 2001, Gable signed an exclusive-brokerage agreement with Ellis to negotiate and consummate leases for office space in the Tower. Among other provisions, the agreement contained the following terms:

> 6. *Agreement to Refer Offers and Inquiries.* During the term of this agreement, Gable agrees to refer to Ellis any and all offers and inquiries by prospective

tenants, and Ellis agrees to investigate and develop such offers and inquiries and to employ its best efforts to lease space in the Tower.

7. *Owner's Reservation to Preempt Broker.* Gable reserves the right to preempt Ellis and deal directly with the prospective tenant with the understanding that, should Gable exercise such right, any commission otherwise payable under this agreement shall remain payable.

8. *Broker's Commission.* Gable agrees to pay Ellis a commission if, within 90 days after the expiration or termination of this agreement, the property is leased or negotiations continue or resume leading to the execution of a lease with any person or entity with whom Ellis has negotiated or to whom the property has been introduced prior to the expiration or termination of this agreement.

In October 2001, Firebridge, a tenant of another property owned by Gable, made a proposal to Gable to rent space in the Tower. In accordance with section 6 of the agreement, Gable referred the inquiry to Barry Farley. Later that month, Firebridge's broker, Joseph Cherry, contacted Gable and requested that Gable negotiate directly with Firebridge because of their existing relationship. Gable agreed and informed Farley that Gable would be exercising its right under section 7 of the Ellis/Gable agreement to negotiate directly with Firebridge but that Gable would need Farley to "work behind the scenes" to bring the deal to a conclusion.

The parties agree on the following chronology of events: On November 19, 2001, Cherry sent Gable a lease proposal which contemplated that Firebridge would lease 140,000 square feet in the Tower and renew its existing lease in the other Gable property. Gable sent the proposal to Farley for his "input." On November 25, 2001, Farley submitted to Gable a "proposal" that he recommended and said should be presented to Firebridge. On November 30, 2001, Farley announced his intention to leave Ellis, and he became essentially *incommunicado* over the course of the next month, failing to respond to e-mails and phone calls. Gable continued to negotiate with

Cherry and Firebridge during this period. Gable sent a letter to Ellis properly exercising its right to terminate their brokerage agreement effective as of February 3, 2002.

At this point, the parties part ways over what happened next. Gable claims that negotiations between Gable and Firebridge regarding the two-pronged lease proposal ended on March 20, 2002 and that the 90-day period during which negotiations must have resumed in order for Ellis to obtain a commission ended on May 3, 2002. Gable asserts that it did not resume negotiations with Firebridge until May 15, 2002, and that these new negotiations "took on a materially different character from the prior negotiations," i.e., that Firebridge would lease 65,000 square feet in the Tower and sublease additional space from the Columbia Redevelopment Agency, one of Gable's existing tenants. On September 6, 2002, Gable and Firebridge signed a lease on these new terms.

Ellis, on the other hand, asserts that negotiations between Gable and Firebridge "continued unabated from November 2001 until the deal was formalized by a June 5, 2002 letter of intent" and that the final lease was consistent with a proposal that Barry Farley had prepared and submitted to Gable in November 2001.

Without reference to the parties' differing presentations of the events or to the 90-day provision of the agreement, the district court held that Columbia law "establishes that a real estate broker earns a commission by actually consummating the transaction or by showing that his or her efforts were the procuring cause of the transaction." It then determined that Ellis was not the procuring cause of the Firebridge lease and granted Gable's motion for summary judgment.

Columbia common law clearly incorporates the doctrine that a contractually retained real estate agent is entitled to a commission if he or she is the "proximate, efficient, and procuring cause of the sale or lease." But it is not a sword that property owners may use to deprive brokers of a contractually guaranteed commission. Rather, it is a shield designed to protect brokers from being stripped of their commissions by sharp-elbowed property owners who fraudulently or in bad faith delay the consummation of a real estate transaction until after a brokerage agreement has ended.

The opposing contentions of the parties are these. Ellis argues that the district court erred by failing to appreciate the difference between Ellis's *contractual* commission claim and a common law claim. That is, asserts Ellis, the district court gratuitously wrote a procuring cause requirement into an unambiguously worded contract.

Gable, on the other hand, argues that, under Columbia law, a procuring cause requirement overshadows all brokerage contracts and prohibits a commission from being awarded unless the claiming broker was the procuring cause.

The relevant terms of the contract at issue in this case leave little room for interpretation regarding the right to a commission after the agreement has ended. Section 8 states that:

> Gable agrees to pay Ellis a commission if, within 90 days after the expiration or termination of this agreement, the property is leased or negotiations continue or resume leading to the execution of a lease with any person or entity with whom Ellis has negotiated [directly or through another broker] . . . prior to the expiration or termination of this agreement.

By its terms, this provision gives Ellis the right to a commission so long as "within 90 days after the termination . . . negotiations continue[d] or resume[d] leading to the execution of a lease." There is nothing in the agreement that requires Ellis to establish that it was the procuring cause of the signed lease. To the contrary, Section 7 of the agreement requires Gable to pay a commission even if Gable itself "preempted" Ellis and conducted all the negotiations itself.

Thus, the factual issues inherent in the differing chronologies argued by the parties must be resolved. If the trier of fact finds that the negotiations that resumed after Ellis's contract expired on May 3, 2002 were, as Gable contends, new and of "a materially different character from the prior negotiations," then Gable would prevail. On the other hand, if the trier of fact found, as Ellis contends, that they were merely a continuation of the same negotiations that Ellis had commenced, then Ellis would prevail.

The proper forum for such a resolution is the district court, to which we remand with instructions to proceed in accordance with this opinion.

AAA BUSINESS BROKERS v. WICKS

Columbia Supreme Court (2004)

AAA Business Brokers (AAA) provides brokerage services to buyers and sellers of businesses, similar to the services of a real estate broker. Arnold Wicks, a Belmont, Columbia businessman, owned Homeguard Security Services (Homeguard), a company that provided antitheft and antiburglary security services for homes and businesses.

David Green, the general manager of Electronic Systems, Inc., a competitor of Homeguard, learned through an acquaintance that Wicks wanted to retire from business and was putting Homeguard up for sale. Green got in touch with Joy Jones, a broker employed by AAA and told her that he was interested in buying a home security business and that he understood that Homeguard was for sale. Based on the tip from Green, Jones contacted Wicks, confirmed that, indeed, he wanted to sell his company, and offered to assist him with the sale.

On behalf of AAA, Jones executed a listing agreement with Wicks for the sale of Homeguard. The contract was a nonexclusive agreement, the term of which was January 25, 2002 through March 24, 2002. It provided that, if Jones produced a ready, willing, and able buyer at $600,000, Wicks would pay AAA a commission of 10% of the sale price. The agreement also contained an "extension clause" that stated, "Seller agrees to pay the full commission to Broker in the event the property is within one year after termination of this agreement sold, traded, or otherwise conveyed to anyone referred to Seller by Broker and with whom Seller negotiated during the term of this agreement."

On January 26, 2002, Jones told Green she had confirmed that Wicks wanted to sell Homeguard – a fact that Green already knew – and directed Green to get in touch with Wicks and negotiate the deal. Green began negotiations with Wicks, but, because of a non-competition agreement in Green's employment contract with Electronic Systems, Inc., Green was constrained to consummate a sale until the end of his non-compete period. Green and Wicks eventually entered into a contract of sale, which closed on July 14, 2002.

Jones's involvement in the transaction consisted of spending about 45 minutes with Wicks on January 25, the day they executed the AAA listing agreement, exchanging two letters regarding the "confidentiality" terms of the transaction, telling two potential buyers, including Green, by telephone that Homeguard was for sale for $600,000, and encouraging them to bid on the property.

Shortly before the close of escrow, AAA submitted a demand in the escrow for a 10% commission. Wicks refused to pay it, asserting that AAA had no right to a commission because AAA was not the procuring cause of the sale. AAA sued for breach of contract, and the trial court, holding that the inquiry began and ended with the "extension clause," entered judgment for AAA.

Wicks appealed, contending that the trial court erred in ruling for AAA because AAA did not establish that it was the efficient procuring cause of the sale. AAA's response is that it was not required to prove that it was the procuring cause because, under the "extension clause" of its contract with Wicks, the evidence established clearly that a sale to a person who AAA had "referred" to Wicks closed within a year after the end of the contract term.

The general rule, adopted by the courts of Columbia, is that the parties to a listing contract are free to frame their agreement in whatever terms they see fit, including a term that makes a broker's right to a commission conditional upon the occurrence of a particular set of circumstances even if the broker is not the procurer of the purchaser. The common law "procuring cause" doctrine – i.e., *a cause originating with a series of events, which, without break in continuity, result in procuring a purchaser ready, willing, and able to buy on the owner's terms* – applies only if the contract between the parties is silent on the issue of consummation of a sale after the expiration of the listing agreement. In other words, "procuring cause" is the default rule.

We agree with the general rule and hold that, because the listing agreement contained an extension clause, AAA need not prove that it was the efficient procuring cause. But that does not end the inquiry. The question remains whether AAA complied with the requirement in the listing agreement that the purchaser be a person who was "*referred* to Seller by Broker."

The term "referred" is nowhere defined in the contract, and the contract does not set out the conditions under which the broker will be deemed to have referred the buyer to the seller. The majority of the authorities in Columbia and other jurisdictions interpreting vague terms in listing agreements such as "refer," "solicit," or "introduce," and similar words have found that such terms necessarily incorporate an unexpressed but inferentially essential requirement that the broker do more than merely send or direct a potential purchaser to a seller. In other words, the majority rule is that, even with the existence of an extension clause, the broker must show that there was at least a *minimal causal connection* between him and the ultimate sale before the broker becomes entitled to a commission.

We adopt the majority rule and hold that a broker seeking to recover under an extension clause must establish some causal connection between the broker's efforts and the eventual sale. This might include negotiations between the parties, facilitating the flow of information, or actual assistance with the closing of the sale. It is not necessary that the broker seeking the commission dominate the transaction, but the broker's participation must be palpable and something more than a mere incidental or contributing influence. A rule that would allow recovery for merely soliciting a buyer without a causal connection with the sale would burden the owner's right to dispose of the property, and we also believe it would be poor public policy to reward brokers with substantial commissions for merely notifying potential buyers of the possibility of a sale without requiring them to exert diligent efforts toward conclusion of the sale.[1]

---

[1] AAA alludes in its briefs to the Guidelines for Arbitrators promulgated by the Columbia Association of Commissioned Brokers and argues that AAA should not be completely foreclosed from claiming at least a portion of the commission for having had *some* involvement in the transaction. The court is cognizant of those Guidelines. They are inapposite here for two reasons: First, this case does not arise in the context of an arbitration. Second, those guidelines deal with disputes *between* brokers competing for the same commission, which is not the case here. An arbitrator has broad discretion under the Guidelines to invoke the equities to apportion the commission between the competing brokers, and the court's holding in this case is not to be read as a rule that

In the present case, AAA's involvement through Jones was at best tangential. She was not involved in any negotiations or the closing of the sale. All she did was tell Green what he already knew and left the rest up to him. Although valid, the extension clause in the AAA contract cannot be interpreted to confer upon a broker a windfall commission so that the broker could simply content herself with sitting back and letting the other parties to the transaction do all the work.

We reverse and remand.

---

infringes upon that discretion. The facts of this case do not lend themselves to apportionment of the commission.

COLUMBIA ASSOCIATION OF COMMISSIONED BROKERS
Guidelines for Arbitrators in Commission Disputes
Between and Among Brokers

It is not uncommon in brokerage transactions that disputes arise between a broker who initiated the series of events leading to consummation of the transaction ("Introducing Broker") and another broker who entered the transaction later and closed the transaction ("Closing Broker"). The Columbia Association of Commissioned Brokers ("CACB"), by whose rules all licensed brokers in the State of Columbia agree to be bound, has promulgated the following guidelines for use by Arbitrators in such disputes. There is no predetermined rule or standard that prescribes which of the brokers is entitled to an arbitration award. All awards are based on the facts of a particular transaction. It often turns on the precise terms of the brokerage contract between the broker and the client. It frequently involves the principles of procuring cause, a doctrine defined and recognized by the courts of Columbia. The following factors reflect common characteristics that arise during the course of such disputes and are intended to serve as guidance to Arbitrators to aid them in reaching their decisions. Not all factors are applicable to all cases, but those that are applicable are to be considered as a whole. The factors are not necessarily weighted equally, nor is the outcome necessarily determined by a simple numerical weighting of the factors in favor of one or the other of the brokers. The Arbitrator has broad discretion, based on the law and the equities, in deciding which broker should prevail or whether the brokers should share in the commission.

GUIDELINES FOR ARBITRATORS IN PROCURING CAUSE CASES

Relevant Factor	Favors Intro Broker	Favors Closing Broker	Comments
1. Buyer is first introduced to the property by the Intro Broker.	Yes		
2. Closing Broker never showed the property.	Yes		
3. Closing Broker wrote and submitted an offer on the property on behalf of the client that was substantially similar to an offer written by Intro Broker within the short period of time.			If the two offers are close in substance or time, this factor moves to neutral.
4. A significant amount of time elapsed between the time Intro Broker showed the property and Closing Broker wrote an offer on the same property.		Yes	
5. Intro Broker provided significant information about the specific property, the neighborhood, value of the property, and other characteristics over a period of time.	Yes		Amount of time spent is not the determining factor; rather, it is the nature and usefulness of the information furnished in inducing the buyer's interest in the property.
6. Intro Broker fails to maintain contact with the client.		Yes	Consideration should be given to whether Intro Broker tried to maintain contact but the client did not respond.

Relevant Factor	Favors Intro Broker	Favors Closing Broker	Comments
7. Client expresses dissatisfaction with Intro Broker's professional abilities or conduct. For example: misrepresentations, lack of disclosure, lack of knowledge of the area and the property, nonresponsiveness to client's inquiries, self-dealing, lack of negotiating skills.		Yes	Where client's dissatisfaction does not rise to the level of "just cause" to end the relationship, the arbitrator can consider awarding the Intro Broker an amount in the nature of a "referral fee."
8. Closing Broker asked about client's relationship with another broker early in the process and determined that there was no existing contractual or exclusive relationship between client and any other broker.		Yes	Brokers failing to inquire about existing relationship do so at the risk of losing the commission. If Closing Broker asked about client's relationship with other broker late in the process, this factor would then favor Intro Broker.

PT-A: SELECTED ANSWER 1

MEMORANDUM

TO: Arbitrator

FROM: Applicant

DATE: February 25, 2014

SUBJECT: Brianna Adams & Associates v. Kustom Spas, Inc.

STATEMENT OF FACTS

Ms. Adams and Mr. Koster of Kustom Spas entered into an agreement for the period of February 1, 2013 through July 31, 2013 whereby Ms. Adams was given a nonexclusive irrevocable right to represent Kustom Spas, Inc. in deals to sell the business. Ms. Adams generated interest in buyers for Kustom Spas by advertising in trade journals, contacting people she knew from prior deals, and by following up with leads Mr. Koster gave her. Once Mr. Baylor of Midvale Pool and Spa Service expressed serious interest, Ms. Adams worked to secure a deal between Mr. Baylor and Mr. Koster by negotiating with Mr. Baylor to offer 1.75 million rather than the 1.5 million that Baylor's appraisal came back at, as well as by arranging for a loan commitment for Mr. Baylor, assisting Mr. Baylor's broker in writing up the 1.75 million dollar offer, working with Mr. Koster's attorney to draft documents, and then opening escrow at Columbia. However, Mr. Koster did not accept the offer and then stopped taking anymore of Ms. Adams' calls. In September, Mr. Smith, a real estate broker, entered into an exclusive agreement with Mr. Koster for the period of September 4, 2013 through October 4, 2013. During this time, he found out Mr. Koster would drop his price and so told Mr. Baylor's broker to make the $1.75 million offer again. The deal closed between the parties on October 23, 2013.

ARGUMENT

1.   Even though the period of contract has ended, Ms. Adams is still entitled to a commission because she was the procuring cause of the sale as the agent who had done substantially everything to effect the sale.

Procuring cause doctrine governs

In Columbia, the "procuring cause" doctrine is the "default rule." AAA Business Brokers. In Columbia, parties are free to contract to determine how a brokerage fee will be paid: the procuring cause rule will not necessarily trump an agreement between the parties. See Ellis Realty. According to AAA Business Brokers, the procuring cause doctrine applies "only if the contract between the parties is silent on the issue of consummation of a sale after the expiration of the listing agreement." Here, while the contract between Koster and Adams had a termination date, it was silent on the issue of consummation of a sale after the expiration date. Rather, their contract states that the broker should be entitled to compensation if seller enters into a contract to sell the property for the 2.5 million asking price or on to her terms agreeable to the seller and the buyer was secured by the broker's efforts. There is no extension clause so there actually is not a definitive time period for when the broker is no longer entitled to commission. As such, Ms. Adams can rely on the procuring cause doctrine to enforce her claim against Mr. Koster and in arguing her claim is superior to Smith's. Since Ms. Adams's efforts did secure the contract that was ultimately entered into, she is entitled to compensation.

Substantially everything to effect the sale

Under the procuring cause doctrine, a salesperson is able to "recover commissions on sales made after the termination of the agency relationship if the salesperson procured the sales through his or her activities prior to the termination of the relationship." Quincy Sales. The purpose of this doctrine is to protect a salesperson who has "done substantially everything necessary to effect the sale." In this case, Ms. Adams' activities, done prior to the termination of the relationship, procured the sale. She had done "substantially everything" to effect the sale. Ms. Adams had first met with Mr. Koster to understand his business and what he hoped to sell it for. She looked at his books, learned about the history, etc. She then secured an appraisal, which valued the business at 1.75 million, including goodwill and going-concern value. She then advertised in trade journals, contacted people she knew, and followed up with acquaintances. The only credible offer ended up being from Mr. Baylor of Midvale Pool and Spa Service in April. Ms. Adams then introduced Baylor and Koster and made arrangements for Baylor's accountants to examine the company's books. After these meetings, Mr. Baylor's appraisal valued the company at 1.5 million. Through Ms. Adams' skill at negotiation, she convinced Mr. Baylor to pay the $1.75, 25 million more than his appraisal valued the business at, and helped to draw up the necessary paperwork to close the deal. She even went so far as to secure financing for him through Vinny Maniscalco Loan Company, because Baylor was having trouble getting the financing for the higher offer price. She opened escrow at Columbia Title Company. Ms. Adams clearly worked to cause the sale between Kustom Spas and Mr. Baylor.

Mr. Koster argued that she is not entitled to the commission because she did him "no good at all" because she was not an effective negotiator. This is a similar argument to NAM's argument in Quincy when NAM argues that Quincy was not the efficient cause of the sale because of the services NAM supplied to DORCO and that these services led to the subsequent sale. However, in this case, as described above, she convinced Mr. Baylor to pay 25 million dollars more than his appraisal came back for. She did this even though there were no other credible offers, so she did not have any leverage in the negotiations. Though Mr. Koster made this sweeping, vague allegation about her lack of effectiveness, he failed to state anything specific she did not do in the course of her representation. In fact, he later finally accepted the offer she wrote up because his wife had died and he was more motivated to take a lower price. In Quincy Sales, the court noted that Sears, NAM's VP, could not "identify anything that Quincy failed to do to bring about the sale [of the machines]" when analyzing NAM's claim that Quincy was not owed full commission. Similarly, Mr. Koster cannot identify anything that Ms. Adams failed to do to bring about the sale. Indeed, she had done "substantially everything to effect the sale" and the only thing that had actually changed was his willingness to sell.

Public Policy and equity favor Ms. Adams

Finally, in support of the position that a commission is due and it is due to Ms. Adams based on Columbia's doctrine of procuring cause, is the court's own justification for the doctrine in Ellis Realty. The court makes clear the policy reasons for this important doctrine. It is meant to be "a shield" and "to protect brokers from being stripped of their commissions by sharp-elbowed property owners who fraudulently or in bad faith delay the consummation of a real estate transaction..." Ms. Adams testified that she knew that she was not including an extension clause in the contract, because Koster had been so tough about even paying her the commission and about her representation being exclusive. She was therefore left to rely on this equitable doctrine that says she will be protected if she had done the work to procure the sale and then is stripped of her commission in bad faith. Here, Koster just kept telling her to negotiate after she brought him the Baylor deal and then, before her contract ran out, stopped taking her calls. He offered her no explanation as to why he stopped taking her calls nor gave her any information about what more she could do to close the deal. He even admits that he has no reason to doubt that she did "all the work she says she did to put together the offer." Yet, because she "didn't make it happen" he refuses to pay her anything. Ms. Adams, as the party who did "all of the work...to put together the offer" is entitled to compensation as the procuring cause of the sale.

2. Ms. Adams, rather than Mr. Smith, is due the full commission, despite his extension clause, because under Columbia law he did not actually "refer" the buyer to the seller since there is not even a minimal causal connection between him and the ultimate sale.

Smith's Extension Clause

As explained above, Columbia allows parties to include extension clauses to contract out of the procuring sale doctrine. In Smith's agreement with Koster, he has an extension clause that provides if seller enters into a binding agreement to sell within a period 180 days after the contract, he is entitled to compensation if he referred the buyer to the seller. In this case, Smith had a valid extension clause and the sale took place within the 180 days it allowed. His contract ended on October 4 and the sale took place at the end of the same month, well within the 180 day period. Smith, on these facts, is in the position to argue that he has a valid claim on the commission. However, for the reasoning below, he still is not entitled to commission, because he did not actually "refer" the buyer to the seller.

Referred

Under Columbia law, the term "referred" means more than a "minimal causal connection between him and the ultimate sale." In this case, there is only a minimal causal connection between Smith and the parties. Smith only told the parties essentially what they already knew, which is similar to what occurred in AAA where the court explained that a broker seeing to "recover under an extension clause must establish some causal connection between the broker's efforts and the eventual sale." In this case, Smith heard that Koster had come close to a deal for the sale with Baylor and was now willing to drop his price based on his losing his wife. After entering into a Seller/Broker Agreement with Koster, Smith went back to Baylor and found out Baylor was still willing to do the deal. As Smith admits, "There wasn't much for me to do" so he just told Baylor to meet with Koster do make the deal. After that, he just let Koster know that Baylor would make the deal. After his, he did nothing else to secure the deal and didn't find out until afterward that it had even occurred. Similar to the agent in AAA, Smith was not involved in any negotiations. Therefore, this is only a minimal causal connection between Smith and the final sale.

The courts in Columbia require that a broker's participation "be palpable and do something more than a mere incidental or contributing influence." On cross-examination, Smith admits that he only met with Koster once, for 45 minutes. This is hardly a palpable impact, especially in contrast to Adams' ongoing, multiple meeting relationship with him. He also admitted that he used the same documentation and loan commitment, with minor updates. Therefore, Smith's influence is much better characterized as "incidental" and Ms. Adams is the actual referring broker who is responsible for the sale. Mr. Smith argues, though, that without his contacts the deal would not have occurred. However, the court seeks to guard against this very situation in AAA when it says that more is required than "merely notifying potential buyers of the possibility of a sale without requiring them to exert diligent efforts toward conclusion of the sale." If Smith were to receive commission in this case, he would be getting a "windfall commission" by just sitting back and "letting the other parties to the transaction do all the work" which is what the Columbia Court specifically found to be unfair in AAA.

3. The commission due to Ms. Adams is the full $175,000 because there are no relevant factors for reducing it.

Guidelines

In Columbia, when a claim arises in the context of arbitration and involves a dispute between brokers competing for the same fee, the Guidelines for Arbitrators are relevant. See AAA Business. Here, both of these criteria are met because the case is in arbitration and Ms. Adams and Mr. Smith are competing for a broker's fee. Therefore, the guidelines are relevant to the arbitrators in reaching their decision. While no one factor is determinative and arbitrators have broad discretion, in this particular case, all of the factors suggest strongly that Ms. Adams has the superior claim and is entitled to full compensation.

Buyer introduced to property by Intro Broker (Ms. Adams)

According to the guidelines, this factors weighs in favor of the intro broker. Here, Ms. Adams introduced Koster and Baylor after Mr. Baylor's broker contacted her.

Closing Broker never showed the property

According to the guidelines, this factor also weighs in favor of the intro broker. Here, by Smith's own admission, Smith only met with Koster once, for about 45 minutes and never showed Koster's property to Baylor. In contrast, Ms. Adams who set up a meeting between the men and arranged for Baylor's accountant to review the books. She also arranged for an appraisal of Koster's business. Therefore, this factor weighs heavily in favor of Ms. Adams.

Closing broker's offer was substantially similar to intro broker's offer within a short period of time

While the rules state that if the offers are close in substance or time, the factor is neutral, Ms. Adams has a strong argument that since the offers are the exact same, she is favored by this rule. In this case, the offers are not substantially similar; they are the exact same offer. They use the same documentation and the same loan commitment. In fact, they also use the same escrow account. Mr. Smith did not have to do any work to prepare the offer; he had no terms to tweak based on any negotiating he carried out. As he said "There wasn't much for me to do" in order to make the sale because Mr. Baylor was willing to make the same offer that Ms. Adams had already drawn up. So Smith used the same loan commitment and the same escrow account. Therefore, while this factor would usually be neutral, in this case, it weighs toward Ms. Adams because the offers are identical.

Significant time between Intro Broker showed property and closing broker wrote offer

This is a factor that could favor Mr. Smith, but, in this case does not because there was not a significant time and Mr. Smith did not write the offer. Here, Mr. Smith did not actually "write" the offer because he just relied on Baylor making the offer that Adams had already written up. Also there were only a few months between the deal.

Intro Broker provided significant information

As already established, Ms. Adams did this through her extensive meetings with the parties. She convinced Baylor to make the offer for more than the appraisal.

Intro broker fails to maintain client contact

While this did occur in the case, the rules state that consideration should be given when broker tries to maintain contact but client stopped responding. This is what occurred in this case. Also, Smith, the closing broker failed to maintain contact with Koster; he did not even know that the offer had gone through until he "ran into Artie Baylor" the day after.

Client expresses dissatisfaction with Intro Broker

Here, Koster expressed dissatisfaction with Adams' negotiating skills. While this does favor the closing broker according to the rules, it does not do so in this case. Here, Koster also expressed dissatisfaction with Smith and actually seeks not to pay either of them. Also, he did not substantiate his claim with any factual basis. Moreover, he ended up taking the deal that Adams wrote up, which undermines his argument extensively.

Closing broker asking about client's other broker relationship

Here, Smith did not ask about the relationship at all, so while this factor could favor Smith, here it does not. It favors Adams because Smith never asked about the prior relationship, despite the fact that the escrow company told him there was an open escrow.

Since the arbitrator has broad discretion in which broker should prevail and what is equitable, in this case, the entire fee should be awarded to Ms. Adams. Mr. Smith's claim should not be enforced under the above analysis and a weighing of the factors all suggest Ms. Adams is the broker who should receive the full payment. Mr. Koster cannot seek to avoid paying either broker by blaming them for doing nothing and then ultimately accepting the fee.

PT-A: SELECTED ANSWER 2

TO: William C. Baines

FROM: Applicant

DATE: February 25, 2014

SUBJECT: Post- Hearing Arbitration Brief

Mr. Baines, I have reviewed your memo and our client, Brianna Adams' case file. I have prepared a draft of a persuasive post-arbitration brief for the arbitrator. I have included it below for your review. Thank You.

I. STATEMENT OF FACTS

Brianna Adams, a licensed broker who specializes in finding buyers for small businesses for sale in Columbia, entered into a six-month listing agreement with Kustom Spas, Inc. to find a buyer for the business at a 10% commission. Ms. Adams expended significant time and effort to procure a ready, willing and able buyer for Kustom Spas. Despite her efforts, a deal was unable to be reached during the six-month listing agreement due to the owner, Mr. Koster's, refusal to accept the buyer's offer based solely on price. However, only a few months after the six-month listing end date, Kustom Spas, using a different broker, Mr. Smith, was sold to the same buyer, based on an offer on the same terms, price and documentation as the original offer that Ms. Adams had procured during her agreement period. Currently, Ms. Adams and Mr. Smith each claim entitlement to a commission of the gross sales price, based on their respective brokerage agreements with Kustom Spas, while Mr. Koster claims that neither is entitled to any commission based on the sale.

II. ARGUMENT

A. MS. ADAMS IS ENTITLED TO A COMMISSION BECAUSE SHE IS THE PROCURING CAUSE OF THE DEAL BETWEEN BAYLOR AND KUSTOM SPAS; AND COMMON LAW APPLIES BECAUSE THERE IS NO PROVISION TO THE CONTRARY IN THE AGREEMENT

The procuring cause rule allows a salesperson, in whatever field of endeavor, to recover commissions on sales made after the termination of the agency relationship if the salesperson procured the sales through his or her activities prior to the termination of the relationship. Quincy Sales v North America Machinery Corp. Moreover, the court in Quincy Sales held that once the agent has put in motion the chain of events that lead to a sale and has done everything in his power and authority to bring about that result, it is irrelevant which party terminated the relationship.

Here, Adams entered into a brokerage agreement with Koster to procure a ready and willing buyer and consummate a sale of his business, Kustom Spas. During her six month term, she did everything that she could to procure a ready and willing buyer.

She met with Koster several times over the course of a six month period. They discussed what Koster wanted to get in price for the property. Adams arranged to have a formal appraisal of the business conducted. This appraisal involved looking at comparables, examining Kustom's books, inquiries into the business' reputation, etc. Adams advertised about the property in trade journals, contacted people she knew from prior deals who had expressed interest in buying a business, and also followed up leads given by Koster himself. The amount of time spent is not determinative but it is the nature and usefulness of the information furnished in inducing the buyer's interest in the property. This is demonstrated by the fact that all of these efforts garnished interest from at least a dozen inquiries, and led to the serious interest of Baylor.

After Baylor entered the picture, Adams entered into intense negotiations with him and his broker. Adams made arrangements for Baylor to obtain a loan that would provide him with the financing to complete the deal. She worked with Koster's attorney to draft transfer documents, and also opened an escrow account at Columbia Title Company. And finally, after Koster refused to accept the deal, after extensive rounds of renegotiation on Adams' and Baylor's part, Adams tried to keep in contact with Koster to make the deal work, but Koster refused to return her phone calls. Despite all of her best efforts, the deal could not be completed during her six month agreement with Koster.

This situation is similar to that in Quincy Sales, where the court determined that the defendant could not identify anything that plaintiff had failed to do to bring about the sale. Plaintiff procured a ready and willing buyer, and it was the defendant who declined. There, the plaintiff negotiated the agreement and prepared the documentation. The deal clearly stated that the plaintiff was to receive commission based on such a sale. Thus, the court held that the plaintiff, as the procuring cause of the sale, was still entitled to receive his commission on the sale even though it was finally consummated after the termination of the agency relationship.

Here, Koster is unable to point to anything that Adams failed to do to bring about the sale. Indeed, he admits to the extensive and significant amount of work that Adams did in fact do on the deal. She engaged in all negotiations and prepared all necessary documents. Moreover, like the defendant in Quincy Sales, it was Foster here who declined to consummate the deal. Finally, the agreement with Adams clearly states that she is entitled to receive a 10% commission of the gross sale of the property, and that she is to receive this commission if the property is sold to a buyer procured through the efforts of Adams.

The procuring cause doctrine does not apply where the agreement between the parties specifically states whether and when post-termination commissions are earned. But here, just as in the Quincy Sales case, the agreement between Koster and Adams does not specify whether and when post-termination commissions are earned. Although

Adams usually includes such a provision, she did not in this case. Accordingly, the procuring cause doctrine does apply.

Thus, despite the fact that the sale between Kustom Spas and Baylor was consummated after the brokerage agreement between Koster and Adams had expired, the common law procuring cause doctrine should apply and allow her to recover the commission that she is rightfully entitled to. Adams procured a ready and willing buyer and did everything she could to bring about the sale to Baylor; the sale didn't occur through no fault of her own, but rather due to Koster declining, and the agreement specifically states that she is entitled to a commission if the sale is consummated with a buyer that she procures.

Thus, Adams is the procuring cause of the sale to Baylor and she is entitled to receive her 10% commission of $175,000.

B. MR. SMITH IS NOT ENTITLED TO A COMMISSION BASED ON THE EXTENSION PROVISION BECAUSE BAYLOR WAS NOT A BUYER "REFERRED TO" KUSTOM SPAS BY SMITH AS SMITH CAN SHOW NO MINIMAL CAUSAL CONNECTION BETWEEN HIM AND THE ULTIMATE SALE

The procuring cause doctrine at common law does not apply to place a restraint on the party's right to contract to determine whether a commission is or is not due under a brokerage agreement. Thus, where the parties include an agreement specifically allowing for a commission to be received after the termination of that agreement then the contract provision control and the procuring cause doctrine does not. Ellis Realty Inc. v Gable Holdings LLC.

Here, the agreement between Smith and Koster included such a provision, stating that Smith would be entitled to his commission if Koster entered into an agreement during the representation or within 180 days to sell the property, if the buyer of the property was a person referred to Koster by Smith.

However, in order to be entitled to receive his commission under this provision, Smith must have "referred" Baylor to Koster.

In AAA Business Brokers v Wicks, the court held that even though a contract contains an extension clause, as is the case here, the inquiry does not end there; the question remains whether the broker complied with the requirement that the purchaser be a person who was "referred to seller by the broker."

The majority of authorities in Columbia and other jurisdictions interpreting vague terms in listing agreements such as "refer" and similar words have found that such terms necessarily incorporate an unexpressed but inferentially essential requirement that the broker do more than merely send or direct a potential purchaser to a seller. In other words, the majority rule is that, even with the existence of an extension clause, the broker must show that there was at least a minimal causal connection between him and the ultimate sale before the broker becomes entitled to a commission.

The court in AAA held that a minimal causal connection can be established by showing negotiations between the parties, facilitating the flow of information, or actual assistance with the closing of the sale. It is not necessary that the broker seeking commission dominate the transaction, but the broker's participation must be palpable and something more than a mere incidental or contributing influence. This is because a rule that would allow recovery for merely soliciting a buyer without a causal connection with the sale would burden the owner's right to dispose of the property, and it would be poor public policy to reward brokers with substantial commissions for merely notifying potential buyers of the possibility of a sale without requiring them to exert diligent efforts towards conclusion of the sale.

In AAA, the court found that the plaintiff failed to demonstrate a sufficient causal connection, stating that all she did was tell the party what he already knew and left everything up to him. Thus, the court was unwilling to allow the broker to collect a commission for simply sitting back and letting the other parties to the transaction do all the work.

This case is similar to AAA, in that no causal connection exists between Smith and the ultimate sale to Baylor, such that he should be entitled to a commission under the extension clause.

Koster himself told Smith that he had come pretty close to a deal with Baylor and that it had fallen through due to price. Thus, this is a similar case to AAA, in that Smith did not procure a new buyer that Koster was unaware of. Koster already knew that Baylor was interested in purchasing the property based on his previous offer. Koster could have easily reached out to Baylor on his own to see if he was still interested in the property; he did not need Smith to accomplish this or the subsequent sale.

Moreover, Smith did absolutely no work with respect to the sale. He called the Columbia Title Company, but did not have to proceed any further because he decided to use the escrow account already set up by Adams for the deal. He admits that he did not stay in contact with the parties because he "assumed Baylor's broker would keep him in the loop"; he did not engage in any negotiations or prepare any documentation. Indeed, he simply used the paperwork from the first round of negotiations with Adams. All of the terms of the agreement were the same and Baylor used the same loan commitment that he acquired through Adams' efforts. Smith admits that there "wasn't much for me to do", stating that he only left a voicemail message for Koster stating that Baylor was going to present him a $1.75 million offer. This was not new to Koster, as Baylor had already once before made this identical offer. Finally, Koster even admits that Smith did nothing at all, except send him an offer that he had already once rejected.

Thus, based on this information it is clear that no causal connection exists between Smith and the ultimate sale. Smith was simply a passive person who informed Koster of an offer of which he was already aware of, and had in fact already rejected. He did not actively participate in the negotiations or prepare any paperwork. He admits that he failed to even keep in contact with the parties. Indeed, he was only aware the sale had even been consummated when he coincidentally ran into Baylor and Baylor told him that the sale had gone through. Thus, he had absolutely no part of the actual closing itself.

Thus, the holding in AAA clearly dictates that Baylor was not "referred to" Koster by Smith. Accordingly, Smith should not be entitled to any commission based on the extension provision in the agreement.

C. MS. ADAMS IS ENTITLED TO HER ENTIRE COMMISSION OF $175,000 BECAUSE THE FACTORS OF THE COLUMBIA ASSOCIATION OF COMMISSIONED BROKERS ("CACB") GUIDELINES FOR ARBITRATORS IN COMMISSION DISPUTES BETWEEN AND AMONG BROKERS WEIGH IN HER FAVOR

Unlike AAA Business Brokers, this dispute arises in the context of an arbitration and is a dispute between brokers competing for the same commission. Thus, the CACB applies. The CACB states that there is no predetermined rule or standard that prescribes which of the brokers is entitled to an arbitration award. The following factors reflect common characteristics that arise during the course of such disputes and are intended to serve as guidance to arbitrators in aiding them to reach a decision as to how to award each or either broker.

An arbitrator has broad discretion under the guidelines to invoke the equities to apportion the commission between competing brokers. Here, almost all of the 8 factors weigh in favor of Ms. Adams and thus she should be entitled to her entire commission of $175,000. As discussed above, Smith is not entitled to receive a commission based on the extension provision because he did not "refer" Baylor to Koster. Moreover, even if Smith were somehow entitled to any sort of a commission, as discussed below, the 8 factors weigh in favor of Adams, and equity should require that she be awarded her full commission, while Smith should not be entitled to share in any of it.

Relevant Factors

1. Buyer is first introduced to the property by the Intro broker

Here, Baylor was first introduced to the property by Adams. Indeed, Baylor's broker responded to one of the ads that Adams had placed in the trade journals about Kustom Spas. Even though Mr. Koster has provided Adams with several leads of potential buyers, Baylor was not one of them.

Thus, this factor weighs in Adams' favor.

2. Closing Broker never showed the property

Here, there is no evidence that Smith ever showed Baylor the property. Indeed, it is likely that Smith did not have to, as Baylor would have likely already been shown the property by Adams during the extensive prior negotiations and meetings that were conducted.

Thus, if Adams had in fact showed Baylor the property, this factor would weigh in Adams' favor.

3. Closing broker wrote and submitted an offer on the property on behalf of the client that was substantially similar to an offer written by the Intro broker within a short period of time

Here, the offer that was submitted by Mr. Smith was identical to the offer submitted by Adams. Indeed, Smith, Adams and Koster all admit that the same paperwork was used, although it had to be slightly updated. Moreover, the same terms of the offer governed;

it was for the same price; the parties made use of the same escrow account that Adams had initially opened for the deal; and Baylor used the same loan commitment from Vinny that Adams was able to obtain for him. Although the documents had to be updated, Smith submitted an offer that was not only substantially similar, but identical, to the offer submitted by Adams. And the offer was submitted only a few months after Adams had first submitted it.

Thus, this factor weighs in Adams' favor.

4. A significant amount of time elapsed between the time the Intro broker showed the property and the Closing broker wrote an offer on the same property

Here, as discussed above, only a few months of time elapsed between the time that Adams showed the property and the time that Smith wrote an offer on the same property.

Thus, this factor weighs in Adams' favor.

5. Intro broker provided significant information about the specific property, the neighborhood, value of the property, and other characteristics over a period of time

Here, Adams expended significant time and effort in providing information about the specific property, the neighborhood, the value and other characteristics over a period of time. She met with Koster several times over the course of a six-month period. They discussed what Koster wanted to get in price for the property. Adams arranged to have a formal appraisal of the business conducted. This appraisal involved looking at comparables, examining Kustom's books, inquiries into the business' reputation, etc. Adams advertised about the property in trade journals, contacted people she knew from prior deals who had expressed interest in buying a business, and also followed up leads given by Koster himself. The amount of time spent is not determinative but it is the nature and usefulness of the information furnished in inducing the buyer's interest in the property. This is demonstrated by the fact that all of these efforts garnished interest from at least a dozen inquiries, and led to the serious interest of Baylor.

Thus, this factor weighs in Adams' favor.

6. Intro broker fails to maintain contact with the client

Here, Adams lost contact with Koster after July 31st, 2013. However, this was only due to his inability to get into contact with Koster. Adams tried several, six or seven times, to contact Koster, but he would not return any of her phone calls. Thus, any failure to maintain communication was not the fault of Adams.

Thus, this factor weighs in Adams' favor.

7. Client expresses dissatisfaction with Intro broker's professional conduct or abilities

Here, although Koster did express dissatisfaction with Adams' work, he also expressed the same with Baylor's. Moreover, his only complaint with Adams was that she did not procure a buyer willing to pay $2.5 million. Koster's dissatisfaction can be regarded not as Adams' incompetence, but rather his unrealistic expectation of what the market would bear and what price his business would command in a sale. Adams presented more than enough information that was accurate and demonstrated that Koster's expectations in price were unrealistic based on the value of his business and market conditions.

Thus, this factor weighs in Adams' favor.

8. Closing broker asked about client's relationship with another broker early in the process and determined that there was no existing contractual or exclusive relationship between the client and any broker

Here, although Smith was unaware of any prior relationship that Koster may have had with another broker, including Adams, this was due to his willful ignorance. Smith did not even make a cursory investigation as to whether any such relationship did or had existed. And based on the fact that Koster specifically told him that he had gotten a previous offer from Baylor that came very close to working out, this should have at least placed Smith on notice that Koster might have used a broker for the transaction at which point he could have inquired into the situation with very little effort. Both Koster and Smith repeatedly state that they did not reveal the relationship with Adams or did not ask about it because they did not see how it mattered. However, this information is clearly relevant given the fact that the agreement with Adams could have given her a right to a commission based on the sale between Baylor and Kustom Spas, as it in fact did.

Thus, this factor weighs in Adams' favor.

Since all, if not the majority of these factors weighs in Adams' favor, equity should require that Adams be awarded her full commission of $175,000. There is nothing to suggest that Smith, equitably, has any right to share in the commission money. Thus, since the escrow account contains only enough money for Adams, she is entitled to the entire $175,000.

III. CONCLUSION

Ms. Adams did all of the work in this deal. She expended significant time and effort to procure a ready, willing and able buyer for Kustom Spas at a price that was fair and indicative of the business' value and what the market would bear. She engaged in all negotiations and prepared all documents. The deal would have gone through, but for Koster's decline of a Baylor's good faith offer. Despite the fact that the deal was not consummated during Adams' six-month agreement, she was the procuring cause of the sale under common law, and as such she is entitled to her commission because the agreement did not specify otherwise to bring it outside the common law scope.

Mr. Smith has sat back and let everyone else do all of the work. The only thing that he did was bring Koster an offer than he had already declined and that he was already well aware of. Mr. Koster did not need Smith to consummate any sale with Baylor. It would be poor public policy to reward brokers with substantial commissions for merely notifying buyers of the possibility of a sale without requiring them to exert diligent efforts towards its conclusion. Thus, any award of a commission to Smith would constitute a windfall commission.

As between Adams and Smith, even if Smith were allowed to collect any type of commission equity would require that in a dispute between them, Adams be awarded the entire amount of the commission. Here, there is only enough money in the escrow account to cover Adams' commission. She is entitled to collect her entire commission and should not have to share this amount with Smith at all. Although an arbitrator has broad discretion under the guidelines to invoke the equities to apportion the commission between competing brokers, all of the factors weigh in favor of Adams and against Smith.

Thus, Adams is entitled to recover the entire $175,000 amount of her 10% commission. The property was sold for $1.75 million and under her agreement she was entitled to a 10% commission; thus $175,000 is her commission. And Smith is not entitled to share in the proceeds of the escrow account.

February 2014

California
Bar
Examination

Performance Test B
INSTRUCTIONS AND FILE

ROCK v. DAVIS

Instructions..

FILE

Memorandum from Penny Andrews to Applicant.....................................

Complaint and Demand for Jury Trial...…......

Answer to Complaint.........…...…..........

Notice of Motion *In Limine*..

Excerpts of Interview Between Penny Andrews and
Criminal Defense Attorney Didi Hill..…..........

Trial Transcript...…...............

ROCK v. DAVIS

INSTRUCTIONS

1. This performance test is designed to evaluate your ability to handle a select number of legal authorities in the context of a factual problem involving a client.

2. The problem is set in the fictional State of Columbia, one of the United States.

3. You will have two sets of materials with which to work: a File and a Library.

4. The File contains factual materials about your case. The first document is a memorandum containing the instructions for the tasks you are to complete.

5. The Library contains the legal authorities needed to complete the tasks. The case reports may be real, modified, or written solely for the purpose of this performance test. If the cases appear familiar to you, do not assume that they are precisely the same as you have read before. Read each thoroughly, as if it were new to you. You should assume that cases were decided in the jurisdictions and on the dates shown. In citing cases from the Library, you may use abbreviations and omit page citations.

6. You should concentrate on the materials provided, but you should also bring to bear on the problem your general knowledge of the law. What you have learned in law school and elsewhere provides the general background for analyzing the problem; the File and Library provide the specific materials with which you must work.

7. Although there are no restrictions on how you apportion your time, you should probably allocate at least 90 minutes to reading and organizing before you begin preparing your response.

8. Your response will be graded on its compliance with instructions and on its content, thoroughness, and organization.

ANDREWS and OUELLETTE

Attorneys at Law

12 Jordan Lane

Grafton, Columbia

MEMORANDUM

TO: Applicant

FROM: Penny Andrews

RE: Rock v. Davis and Bond

DATE: February 27, 2014

Our firm represents Gerald Rock in an action against detectives of the Grafton City Police Department for violation of his civil rights. Defense counsel filed a motion *in limine* to have certain evidence excluded at trial as hearsay. I need to prepare our position, in anticipation of defendants' argument supporting their motion.

Before I write my reply, please draft an objective memorandum that identifies and discusses the arguments, resolution of which will determine whether the evidence in question should be admitted. Ultimately, motions *in limine* are won or lost on how well we use the facts. Therefore, your objective memorandum should relate specific facts to the potential arguments and conclude how your analysis establishes whether the evidence will be admitted.

United States District Court

Southern District of Columbia

Gerald Rock,
 	
          Plaintiff
 	
v.
 	
Detective Richard Davis
and Detective Thomas Bond,
 	
          Defendants.
	C.A. No. 2182
	
	COMPLAINT AND
	DEMAND FOR JURY TRIAL

JURISDICTION

1. Plaintiff, Gerald Rock, is a citizen of the State of Columbia and a resident of Grafton City, Columbia.

2. Jurisdiction is based on 42 U.S.C. §§ 1983 and 1988. The amount in controversy exceeds $75,000.00 excluding costs and attorneys' fees.

CLAIM I

3. Defendant, Detective Richard Davis, was and is an employee of the Grafton City Police Department.

4. Defendant, Detective Thomas Bond, was and is an employee of the Grafton City Police Department.

5. On August 29, 2011, Plaintiff was lawfully present in the Grafton City Courthouse in the State of Columbia.

6. While at the Grafton County Courthouse on August 29, 2011, Plaintiff was unlawfully and without just cause, falsely arrested and imprisoned by Defendants.

7. Each Defendant acted maliciously, willfully and wantonly, and outside the scope of his jurisdiction, although under color of law, and violated the right of Plaintiff to

be free from unreasonable search and seizure, from warrantless search and seizure, and from summary punishment without trial and due process of law.

8. Defendants, by their conduct, intentionally, willfully and without justification, and under color of law, did deprive Plaintiff of his rights, privileges and immunities secured to him by the Constitution and the laws of the United States, and by 42 U.S.C. §§ 1983 and 1988.

CLAIM II

9. Plaintiff realleges and incorporates by reference the facts contained in paragraphs 1 through 8.

10. That after the accosting of Plaintiff by Defendants, Plaintiff was falsely arrested and imprisoned while awaiting trial for approximately nine months by the City of Grafton.

CLAIM III

11. Plaintiff realleges and incorporates the facts contained in paragraphs 1 through 10.

12. After the false arrest, imprisonment and violation of his civil rights, Plaintiff was maliciously prosecuted by the Defendants in Grafton County Superior Court.

13. Defendants knew the prosecution was false when commenced.

14. The false charge was eventually dismissed by Judge Charles Heffernan June 11, 2012.

WHEREFORE, Plaintiff prays judgment as follows:

1. General and special damages in the amount of fifteen million dollars ($15,000,000);

2. Punitive and exemplary damages in an amount that this Court shall consider to be just and fair;

3. Attorneys' fees in an amount that this Court shall consider just and fair; and

4.   Costs and disbursements of this action and such other and further relief as this Court may deem just and proper.

ANDREWS and OUELLETTE

By: ____*Penny Andrews*_____
   Penny Andrews
   Attorney for Plaintiff

   Dated: June 3, 2013

United States District Court

Southern District of Columbia

Gerald Rock,
 	
    Plaintiff
 	
v.
 	
Detective Richard Davis
and Detective Thomas Bond,
 	
    Defendants.
	C.A. No. 2182
	
	ANSWER TO COMPLAINT

ANSWER

1. Defendants deny each and every allegation in paragraphs 1 and 6-14, except admit that Plaintiff was arrested by Defendants, subsequently tried and acquitted.

2. Defendants admit to the allegations in paragraphs 3-5.

3. Defendants lack sufficient information and belief of the allegations in paragraph 1 and therefore deny each and every allegation.

4. Defendants deny each and every allegation in paragraph 2, except admit that Plaintiff purports to invoke the jurisdiction of this court as stated therein.

FIRST AFFIRMATIVE DEFENSE

5. The complaint fails to state a claim upon which relief can be granted.

SECOND AFFIRMATIVE DEFENSE

6. Any injury alleged to have been sustained resulted from Plaintiff's own culpable or negligent conduct and/or the intervening culpable or negligent conduct of others and was not the proximate result of any act of Defendants.

THIRD AFFIRMATIVE DEFENSE

7.   There was probable cause for Plaintiff's arrest and prosecution.

FOURTH AFFIRMATIVE DEFENSE

8.   Defendants have not violated any clearly established constitutional or statutory right of which a reasonable person should have known, and therefore are protected by qualified immunity.

FIFTH AFFIRMATIVE DEFENSE

9.   At all times relevant to the incident, Defendants acted reasonably and in the proper and lawful exercise of their discretion.

WHEREFORE, Defendants request judgment dismissing the complaint in its entirety, together with the costs and disbursements of this action and such other and further relief as the Court may deem just and proper.

_____*Mary Lynch*_____

Mary Lynch
Attorney for Defendants

Dated: July 5, 2013

United States District Court

Southern District of Columbia

Gerald Rock,
 	
        Plaintiff
 	
v.
 	
Detective Richard Davis
and Detective Thomas Bond,
 	
        Defendants.
	C.A. No. 2182
	
	NOTICE OF MOTION
	IN LIMINE

PLEASE TAKE NOTICE that, upon all previous papers and proceedings in this matter, the undersigned will move this Court at the Courthouse located at 677 Pearl Street, Columbia, on March 6, 2014 at 9:00 a.m., or as soon thereafter as counsel can be heard, for an order:

> Excluding as hearsay, evidence of all transcripts or testimony concerning the prior testimony of the witness Joe Watts in the criminal trial of Plaintiff, out of which Plaintiff alleges his cause of action arose.

_____*Mary Lynch*_____

Mary Lynch
Attorney for Defendants

Dated: February 26, 2014

EXCERPTS OF INTERVIEW BETWEEN PENNY ANDREWS

AND CRIMINAL DEFENSE ATTORNEY DIDI HILL

March 1, 2013

. . . . .

HILL: Thanks for agreeing to meet with me, Penny.

ANDREWS: No problem. So, I understand you want to talk about a client of yours.

HILL: Yes, actually a former client, I guess. I know you'll have to talk directly to him, but he asked me to run this by you first. He's a little wary of the justice system at the moment.

ANDREWS: No problem.

HILL: I represented Gerald Rock in a criminal matter. He was charged with shooting someone, was acquitted, and now I think he may have a good civil claim against two of the police detectives involved.

ANDREWS: You aren't interested in taking it?

HILL: Not really. You know my partner died last year and he handled the civil stuff in the office. I am pretty much sticking to the criminal side.

ANDREWS: Okay, so tell me what happened?

HILL: On August 29, 2011, a shooting took place at the Grafton County Courthouse. Apparently a stray bullet struck and wounded a fifteen-year-old girl, Margaret Terry.

ANDREWS: Was this at night?

HILL: No. It was about 5:00 p.m.

ANDREWS: Who was this Margaret Terry?

HILL: That's part of the tragedy. She was just an innocent bystander who never saw the person who shot her.

ANDREWS: Okay, so then what happened?

HILL: The shooting was investigated by a couple of detectives named Richard Davis and Thomas Bond. The story is that someone called 911 and eventually Davis and

Bond were assigned to investigate. Bond went to the scene to interview any witnesses and Davis went to pick up a guy named Joe Watts.

ANDREWS: Why Watts?

HILL: The detectives claimed later that the 911 caller, anonymous of course, said he might have seen Watts at the scene.

ANDREWS: I assume Watts has issues with the police?

HILL: Yeah, mostly petty stuff, but he was clearly on the police radar screen.

ANDREWS: So, then what happened?

HILL: Bond went to the crime scene and Davis found Watts and took him to the police station, where he interviewed him.

ANDREWS: Let me guess. He denied everything.

HILL: Close. He admitted he was near the courthouse at the time of the shooting, but denied being involved. The problem was he identified Rock as one of the shooters. Rock was then arrested and he called me.

ANDREWS: Go on.

HILL: The grand jury indicted Rock, charging him with various counts of assault, reckless endangerment, and criminal possession of a weapon.

ANDREWS: Did Watts testify at the grand jury?

HILL: Yes, and he again said my client was one of the shooters.

ANDREWS: What happened at trial?

HILL: Watts recanted his prior statements, both to Davis and the grand jury, identifying Rock as a shooter. Long story short, my client was released approximately nine months after his arrest.

ANDREWS: I assume this surprised you.

HILL: The renunciation? No. All along we claimed Davis and Bond coerced Watts into falsely accusing Rock as one of the shooters on the day of the shooting, and then pressured Watts into repeating the false accusation before the grand jury.

ANDREWS: So what is the story with Watts?

HILL: At trial, Watts, the sole witness against my client by the way, recanted under oath and in open court before the jury, and stated that the detectives had forced him to falsely testify against my guy.

ANDREWS: The District Attorney must not have been happy. Did the DA get in the grand jury testimony or try to rehabilitate Watts in any way?

HILL: The District Attorney made no effort to rehabilitate him with his grand jury testimony, despite prompting from the Court. I've got the trial transcript right here.

ANDREWS: Thanks. Why would the DA do nothing?

HILL: You're never sure what the other side is thinking, but my best guess is that he knew the case was lost and he just wanted it to end. There certainly were a lot of dirty looks between the DA and the two detectives. I think the DA just wanted to cut his losses before Watts could say anything more that could subject the city to civil liability.

ANDREWS: Okay, so back to Davis questioning Watts. After Watts fingered your guy, what happened?

HILL: After interviewing Watts, Davis called Bond at the crime scene. Davis told Bond that Rock was a suspect in the investigation and should be apprehended, which he was.

ANDREWS: Did Davis and Bond testify at trial?

HILL: No, neither testified at the criminal trial.

ANDREWS: Who signed the criminal complaint?

HILL: Detective Davis.

ANDREWS: You said your theory all along was that Watts was coerced. What led you to that theory?

HILL: Well, of course, to begin with you look at Watts's motivation. He was at the scene. He had a criminal record; given, it was minor. He had to be scared and was looking for a way to get Davis off his back. But then something else happened.

ANDREWS: What?

HILL: I got a phone call from Watts on my answering machine. He said he needed to talk to me. I called him back and he told me that he had been pressured to identify someone, so he did. He denied ever seeing Rock shoot a gun that day. I've got transcripts of those conversations I can give you.

ANDREWS: Thanks. When did this happen?

HILL: It was a couple of days after the grand jury indicted Rock.

ANDREWS: Where is Watts now?

HILL: Well, that's a problem. Rock tried to contact Watts to thank him for being a stand-up guy, but he found out Watts died last week in a liquor store robbery.

. . . . .

STATE OF COLUMBIA

GRAFTON COUNTY
SUPERIOR COURT

State of Columbia, v. Gerald Rock	Criminal Division 2011-2341

TRIAL TRANSCRIPT

BY THE DISTRICT ATTORNEY: The State calls Joe Watts.

. . . . .

DIRECT EXAMINATION OF **JOE WATTS** BY THE DISTRICT ATTORNEY:

. . . . .

DA: Are you now telling us you did not see the defendant shoot the victim?

WATTS: Yes.

DA: After you were arrested, did you give a statement to the police?

WATTS: Yes, sir.

DA: What did you tell the police?

WATTS: I told them I had nothing to do with it.

DA: Did you give them any other statements?

WATTS: Yes, sir.

DA: What else did you tell them?

WATTS: What happened -- I told them what they wanted to hear, sir.

DA: What was that?

WATTS: That I had nothing to do with it.

DA: What did you -- what did you think they wanted to hear?

WATTS: Who did the shooting.

DA: Did you tell them?

WATTS: Yes.

DA: Who did you tell them did the shooting?

WATTS: I said I saw one of them and it was Gerry Rock.

DA: You told them you saw defendant do the shooting?

WATTS: Yes, sir.

DA: Why did you testify to that?

WATTS: Because I was forced under pressure, sir.

DA: Were you lying then?

WATTS: Yes, sir.

DA: I have no further questions, your honor.

. . . . .

CROSS-EXAMINATION BY DEFENSE COUNSEL DIDI HILL:

HILL: Is it your testimony here in Court under oath that you did not see Mr. Rock with a gun. Is that correct?

WATTS: Yes, ma'am.

HILL: Is it your testimony here under oath that you did not see Mr. Rock place a gun in the car. Is that correct?

WATTS: I didn't see him do anything like that.

HILL: But did you ever tell that to the police?

WATTS: Yes, ma'am.

HILL: When you were questioned by the police, did you feel pressured by the police?

WATTS: Yes, ma'am.

HILL: Tell us how you felt pressured by the police?

WATTS: Because they said my mom's house could get –

BY THE DISTRICT ATTORNEY: Objection.

. . . . .

BY DEFENSE COUNSEL:

HILL: You called my office the day after your grand jury appearance. Is that correct?

WATTS: Yes

HILL: You left a voice message?

WATTS: Yes.

HILL: I then returned your phone call. Correct?

WATTS: Yes.

BY DEFENSE COUNSEL: Your honor, at this point we would like to introduce what have been previously marked as Defense Exhibits 1 and 2. They are transcripts of the audio recordings of both the voice message left by Mr. Watts and our subsequent phone conversation. The prosecution has previously stipulated to the accuracy of these recordings.

BY THE COURT: I think we should excuse the jury for a few minutes. Bailiff, will you please escort the jury back to the jury room? . . . . . The jury has been removed, so let's hear those tapes. . . . Well, now that we have heard those tapes — let me just say for the record that the jury is still out of the courtroom -- let me ask the government, where are you going after this witness?

DA: This is our last witness.

THE COURT: Do you have any other evidence at all?

DA: No, your honor.

THE COURT: Then if defense counsel is done with Mr. Watts, the prosecution will rest?

DA: Yes.

THE COURT: I assume the defense is done with Mr. Watts. Correct?

HILL: Yes.

THE COURT: And the prosecution rests? Your only witness is Watts?

DA: Yes.

THE COURT: Let me go out on a limb here now and guess that defense counsel wants to make a motion for a directed verdict. Is that safe to say?

HILL: Yes, your honor.

THE COURT: Granted.

DEFENSE EXHIBIT 1

TRANSCRIPT OF VOICE MAIL MESSAGE LEFT BY JOE WATTS TO DEFENSE ATTORNEY DIDI HILL, SEPTEMBER 9, 2011

BY JOE WATTS: Um, you know um, this is Joe Watts. I'm the guy who was arrested and the police took me down to the station. I, um, am the one who fingered Gerry for the shooting. I told them the wrong story. They were trying to blame me. They said that I needed to confess or tell them who did it. They were trying to use my story against my friend and it's not true. Now I just testified at the grand jury and I get the same pressure before I go in and, um, I lied again. I told them it was Gerry that did it. So I just want to correct my story because the police told it wrong. Can you call me back, please?

DEFENSE EXHIBIT 2

TRANSCRIPT OF TELEPHONE CONVERSATION BETWEEN JOE WATTS AND DEFENSE ATTORNEY DIDI HILL, SEPTEMBER 9, 2011

. . . . .

HILL: So you saw someone in your backyard shoot toward the courthouse?

WATTS: Yeah.

HILL: Was it Gerald who fired the gun?

WATTS: I never even saw him. I never saw him there. I couldn't even see him down the block, even if he was down the block.

HILL: Now I'm confused. You didn't see who?

WATTS: Um, Gerry.

HILL: He wasn't in the backyard?

WATTS: Nah.

HILL: Did you ever see Gerald Rock fire a shot?

WATTS: No.

. . . . .

HILL: Okay, just so I make sure that there's nothing bad going on. Are you being threatened by anybody? Is anyone telling you to say something?

WATTS: Yes.

HILL: Tell me about that.

WATTS: The detective, ma'am.

HILL: What did the detective say?

WATTS: He said, "Oh, I know what happened -- blah, blah, blah," and told me, "You better start talking -- blah, blah, blah," and he slapped me.

HILL: Really?

WATTS: Yeah.

. . . . .

HILL: Okay. Are you being threatened at all -- I just have to ask you this -- by Gerald?

WATTS: No.

February 2014

California
Bar
Examination

Performance Test B

LIBRARY

ROCK v. DAVIS

LIBRARY

Selected Provisions of the Federal Rules of Evidence……………………………..

Hannah v. City of Overland
United States Court of Appeals, Fifteenth Circuit (1986)…………………………..

United States v. Cabrera
United States Court of Appeals, Fifteenth Circuit (2004)…………………....……

United States v. Bryce
United States Court of Appeals Fifteenth Circuit (2000)…………………………

Selected Provisions of the Federal Rules of Evidence

Rule 801. Definitions That Apply to This Article; Exclusions from Hearsay

(a) Statement. "Statement" means a person's oral assertion, written assertion, or nonverbal conduct, if the person intended it as an assertion.

(b) Declarant. "Declarant" means the person who made the statement.

(c) Hearsay. "Hearsay" means a statement that:

(1) the declarant does not make while testifying at the current trial or hearing; and

(2) a party offers in evidence to prove the truth of the matter asserted in the statement.

. . . . .

Rule 802. The Rule Against Hearsay

Hearsay is not admissible unless any of the following provides otherwise:

- a federal statute;
- these rules; or
- other rules prescribed by the Supreme Court.

. . . . .

Rule 804. Exceptions to the Rule Against Hearsay -- When the Declarant Is Unavailable as a Witness

(a)   Criteria for Being Unavailable. A declarant is considered to be unavailable as a witness if the declarant: . . . . .

(4)   cannot be present or testify at the trial or hearing because of death or a then-existing infirmity, physical illness, or mental illness; or . . . .

(b)   The Exceptions. The following are not excluded by the rule against hearsay if the declarant is unavailable as a witness:

(1)   *Former Testimony.* Testimony that:

(A) was given as a witness at a trial, hearing, or lawful deposition, whether given during the current proceeding or a different one; and

(B)   is now offered against a party who had -- or, in a civil case, whose predecessor in interest had -- an opportunity and similar motive to develop it by direct, cross, or redirect examination.

. . . . .

(3) *Statement Against Interest.* A statement that:

   (A) a reasonable person in the declarant's position would have made only if the person believed it to be true because, when made, it was so contrary to the declarant's proprietary or pecuniary interest or had so great a tendency to invalidate the declarant's claim against someone else or to expose the declarant to civil or criminal liability; and

   (B) is supported by corroborating circumstances that clearly indicate its trustworthiness, if it is offered in a criminal case as one that tends to expose the declarant to criminal liability.

. . . . .

Rule 807. Residual Exception

(a) In General. Under the following circumstances, a hearsay statement is not excluded by the rule against hearsay even if the statement is not specifically covered by a hearsay exception in Rule 803 or 804:

   (1) the statement has equivalent circumstantial guarantees of trustworthiness;

   (2) it is offered as evidence of a material fact;

   (3) it is more probative on the point for which it is offered than any other evidence that the proponent can obtain through reasonable efforts; and

   (4) admitting it will best serve the purposes of these rules and the interests of justice.

(b) Notice. The statement is admissible only if, before the trial or hearing, the proponent gives an adverse party reasonable notice of the intent to offer the statement and its particulars, including the declarant's name and address, so that the party has a fair opportunity to meet it.

Hannah v. City Of Overland

United States Court of Appeals, Fifteenth Circuit (1986)

Plaintiff, David Hannah, filed suit under 42 U.S.C. § 1983, against the City of Overland and two members of its police force alleging that he was arrested and detained without probable cause on a capital murder charge and that the arresting officers used unreasonable and excessive force in arresting him. The District Court found in favor of all defendants. On appeal Hannah contends that the District Court erred in excluding the deposition testimony of two persons not parties to the action.

Robert "Red" Musgrove was murdered on June 18, 1981, in the City of Overland. Evidence was introduced that a life insurance policy on the victim's life had been purchased just prior to the murder, and that the named beneficiary under the policy was the victim's estranged wife, Sharon Musgrove. Mrs. Musgrove's boyfriend at the time of the murder was David Hannah.

The two police officer defendants interviewed Danny Beede as part of their investigation into the murder. Beede told the police officers that on June 27, 1981, he was drinking at a local bar with David Hannah. According to Beede, Hannah had told him that he had shot a man four times in the chest with a .38 from an alley, and had silenced the shots by placing a baby bottle nipple over the revolver. Based in large part on Beede's statement, a grand jury indictment was obtained and Hannah was arrested and charged with capital murder.

As part of its continuing investigation following Hannah's arrest, the Overland police interviewed Robert Mesko. During that interview Mesko provided evidence corroborating Beede's version of his conversation with Hannah.

Subsequent to the police interview, Hannah's defense counsel deposed Mesko. Overland's city prosecutor was present at the taking of that deposition.

Hannah was detained in the Overland jail for approximately eleven months until the criminal charge was dropped on June 25, 1982. According to the city prosecutor's office, the capital murder charge was dropped when Danny Beede refused to testify or cooperate with the prosecutor unless he was given some kind of "deal" regarding a prison sentence he then was serving in Ohio on an unrelated conviction.

Citing Federal Rule of Evidence 804(b)(1), Hannah sought to introduce the deposition testimony of Mesko. Mesko stated in his deposition that he felt he was "pressured" and "threatened" by Overland police officers to cooperate in the Musgrove investigation and to implicate Hannah in the murder. Hannah sought to admit the deposition into evidence to establish defendants' bad faith in arresting and detaining him. Mesko himself died just before this action was commenced. Hannah's counsel stated at trial that the deposition "will show that the police did their damnedest to put David Hannah in jail in spite of the fact that Mesko said he wasn't guilty...." Hannah argues that the jury reasonably could infer that police officers who were willing to threaten third parties to gain evidence against Hannah acted in bad faith.

We affirm the District Court's exclusion of the deposition testimony of Mesko. Under Rule 804(b)(1), former deposition testimony taken in another proceeding is not excluded by the hearsay rule if, in a civil action, a "predecessor in interest had an opportunity and *similar motive* to develop the testimony by direct, cross, or redirect examination." (emphasis added)

The proper approach, therefore, in assessing similarity of motive under Rule 804(b)(1) must consider whether the party resisting the offered testimony at a pending proceeding had at a prior proceeding an interest of substantially similar intensity to prove (or disprove) the same side of a substantially similar issue. The nature of the two proceedings—both what is at stake and the applicable burden of proof—and, to a lesser extent, the cross-examination at the prior proceeding—both what was undertaken and what was available but forgone—will be relevant though not conclusive on the ultimate issue of similarity of motive.

An attorney from the Overland prosecutor's office represented the State at the depositions. There were no representatives on behalf of any of the defendants herein present. Assuming *arguendo* that the State was a "predecessor in interest" of the defendants in the present action -- a proposition that is by no means clear -- the prosecutor did have an "opportunity" to develop the testimony of Mesko. We do not believe, however, that he had a "similar motive" to develop his testimony.

When the deposition was taken, Hannah already had been indicted by a grand jury for capital murder, and was awaiting trial in the criminal prosecution. The State's case rested in large part on the testimony of Danny Beede. The fact Mesko testified he was "threatened" and "pressured" by the police to implicate Hannah in the murder was of little, if any, concern to the State at that time. The State apparently thought it had sufficient credible evidence to prove Hannah's guilt beyond a reasonable doubt. The testimony of Mesko posed little danger, if any, to the State's case against Hannah. We do not believe that the State had any significant motive, much less a "similar" motive, to develop the testimony of Mesko regarding threats by the police. It follows that the deposition testimony of Mesko would not have been admissible under Rule 804(b)(1).

Affirmed.

United States v. Cabrera

United States Court of Appeals, Fifteenth Circuit (2004)

Luis G. Cabrera was found guilty of two counts of first-degree murder and now appeals.

In January, 1996, a pedestrian discovered the bodies of Brandon Saunders and Vaughn Rowe in a wooded area of Rockford National Park. Investigators eventually regarded the defendant, Luis Cabrera, as a suspect. Several items of physical evidence linked Cabrera to the victims, including a belt seized from the Cabrera residence.

Dr. Richard Callery testified that during the autopsy of Mr. Rowe he observed an injury that resembled the imprint of a belt buckle. The government then introduced expert testimony that drew a connection between the patterned injuries observed on Rowe and the belt seized from Cabrera's residence. Finally, regarding the belt, Milly Mathis testified at trial that she met Cabrera in 1994 and had sporadic sexual encounters with him over the course of several years. Mathis testified that she was familiar with Cabrera's clothing style and identified a distinctive belt seized from his residence as one that he likely would have worn. She also stated, however, that she did not specifically recognize the belt.

Several months after his conviction, Cabrera moved for a new trial based on post-trial, out-of-court statements made by Milly Mathis. In statements given to Cabrera's counsel after trial, Mathis purported to recant her testimony and claimed that she had been coerced into giving perjured testimony at trial. At an evidentiary hearing on the motion for a new trial conducted by the trial judge, Mathis declined to testify on grounds of self-incrimination. Thus, she became "unavailable" as a witness.

Cabrera's attorneys then sought to introduce Mathis' post-conviction statements. Those statements of the unavailable declarant, Mathis, constitute hearsay because they were offered to prove the truth of their contents. The question before the trial judge, therefore, was whether the post-conviction statements should be admitted under either of two exceptions to the hearsay rule: Federal Rule of Evidence 804(b)(3) that pertains to statements against interest, and Rule 807, the "residual exception" relating to statements not covered by other exceptions "but having equivalent circumstantial guarantees of trustworthiness."

The trial judge ruled that Cabrera failed to carry this burden sufficiently to justify a new trial because the hearsay statements were inadmissible and the other evidence at the hearing suggested that it was Mathis' recantation, and not her trial testimony, that was false. Thus, the key issue is whether the trial judge abused his discretion in refusing to admit Mathis' post-conviction statements in evidence.

Hearsay statements are generally not admissible unless the statement falls within a recognized exception to the hearsay rule. Rule 804(b)(3) allows the admission of a statement against interest if the declarant is unavailable to testify as a witness. Rule 804(b)(3) also imposes two conditions to the admissibility of hearsay evidence in addition to the declarant's unavailability. First, a statement against interest will be admissible only if it so far tended to subject the declarant to civil or criminal liability that a reasonable person in the declarant's position would not have made the statement unless the declarant believed it to be true. Second, a statement tending to expose the declarant to criminal liability and offered to exculpate the accused may be admitted only if corroborating circumstances clearly indicate the trustworthiness of the statement.

Mathis became unavailable to testify when she invoked her Fifth Amendment privilege at the evidentiary hearing. Mathis' statement that she did not testify truthfully at trial was against her penal interest because it amounted to a squarely self-inculpatory confession. A reasonable person would know that admitting to giving false testimony would subject the person to criminal liability for perjury. In addition, the government had not offered Mathis immunity from any potential perjury charges and had even threatened to bring perjury charges against her if she recanted her trial testimony.

Mathis' statements, nonetheless, fail the test of admissibility under Rule 804(b)(3) because they lack corroborating evidence. The trial judge also focused on the fact that Mathis' recanting statement was made more than six months after she testified at trial. Mathis corresponded with Cabrera numerous times before meeting with his attorney. Thus, Mathis' recantation was not spontaneous, but was part of her attempt to build a relationship with Cabrera. The trial judge concluded that such a large temporal gap and lack of spontaneity did not support the admissibility of the statement.

The District Court did not abuse its discretion by finding that Mathis' statement was inadmissible under Rule 804(b)(3). Cabrera failed to meet his burden of clearly demonstrating with corroborating circumstances the trustworthiness of the statement.

Mathis' statements also were not admissible under Rule 807. That Rule provides an exception to the hearsay rule where a statement has sufficient circumstantial guarantees of trustworthiness if the court determines (1) the statement is offered as evidence of a material fact, (2) the statement is more probative on the point for which it is offered than any other evidence which the proponent can procure through reasonable efforts, and (3) the general purposes of these rules and the interests of justice will best be served by admission of the statement into evidence.

The requirements are construed narrowly so that the exception does not swallow the hearsay rule. Mathis' post-trial statements fail to satisfy the requirement that the evidence have circumstantial guarantees of trustworthiness for the same reasons that they were not admissible under Rule 804(3)—they were not supported by sufficient corroborating evidence. In addition, excluding the evidence does not pose a great risk of miscarriage of justice, because Mathis' trial testimony was weak and related to only one small link among several implicating Cabrera in the crime. The District Court did not abuse its discretion by denying Cabrera's motion for a new trial because it had no admissible evidence on which to base the granting of a new trial.

Affirmed.

United States v. Bryce

United States Court of Appeals, Fifteenth Circuit (2000)

Ewan Bryce appeals from the judgment of the United States District Court convicting him, after a jury trial, of (i) conspiracy to possess with intent to distribute, and distribution of, cocaine; and (ii) possession with intent to distribute, and distribution of, cocaine.

In 1997, federal law enforcement officers in Connecticut conducted surveillance of several persons suspected of narcotics trafficking, including the appellant, Ewan Bryce, and his co-defendant, Darren Johnson. On August 5 and 6, 1997, agents intercepted and recorded a number of telephone conversations, eight of which are relevant to this case: seven calls between Bryce and Johnson (the Bryce–Johnson tapes), and one between Johnson and another individual, Edwin Gomez (the Johnson–Gomez tape).

During their conversations, Bryce and Johnson used guarded and coded phrases to arrange a transaction in which Bryce would sell powder cocaine to Johnson for $22,500 per kilogram. In their initial call on August 5, Bryce claimed to possess a quantity of what he called "straight." Johnson expressed interest in buying some of this "straight," and Bryce told Johnson to call him back later that night, presumably to arrange a meeting. But when Johnson called Bryce's cellular phone, there was no answer.

In a call early the next morning, August 6, Bryce told Johnson that he had already "let off" "like 6 of 'em . . . at 22–5." Approximately three hours later, Johnson telephoned Gomez and informed him, in less cryptic language, that Bryce was selling "straight powder" for "deuce deuce" and had "off'ed 7 of 'em yesterday [August 5]." Johnson and Gomez expressed concern that the price being quoted would depress the price in other transactions.

After discussing matters with Gomez, Johnson called Bryce back and said he would buy "two," to which Bryce responded: "Okay. Alright I'm gonna, um, call you back then." Two minutes later, before Bryce could return Johnson's call, Johnson called Bryce again and told him that he would actually buy more than two, so long as Bryce was indeed selling "straight." They agreed to meet at Bryce's home in fifteen minutes. That meeting apparently never happened, however, because Bryce called Johnson several hours later to say that he really only had "one" left, and that he did not "really wanna get rid of this one," but Johnson (by now quite put out) pleaded with Bryce to sell the "one" to him. Reluctantly, Bryce agreed, and they arranged to meet later that day. It is apparent that this meeting also never happened, because Johnson called Bryce on August 11 and asked him whether he still had "it." Bryce said he did, and they again agreed to meet.

On August 26, 1997, federal agents arrested Johnson and another individual, one Michael McCausland. The next day, Bryce terminated the service on his pager; less than a month later, he began using a new cellular telephone. Soon thereafter, Bryce was also arrested.

Bryce and Johnson were charged in a two-count indictment. Count One alleged that the two conspired together and with others to possess with intent to distribute, and to distribute, cocaine; Count Two alleged that between, on, or about August 5 and 6, 1997, Bryce possessed with intent to distribute, and distributed, cocaine.

A jury convicted Bryce on both counts. The district court then sentenced Bryce to 124 months of imprisonment on each count (to be served concurrently) and five years of supervised release, plus a fine and an assessment.

Bryce challenges his conviction on the ground that the district court erred in admitting certain hearsay evidence—specifically, the Johnson–Gomez tape, on which Johnson repeats Bryce's claim that he has cocaine for sale and has already distributed some to others. The district court admitted the tape pursuant to the catch-all exception to the hearsay rule, Fed.R.Evid. 807, which permits admission of hearsay if (i) it is particularly trustworthy; (ii) it bears on a material fact; (iii) it is the most probative evidence addressing that fact; (iv) its admission is consistent with the rules of evidence and advances the interests of justice; and (v) its proffer follows adequate notice to the adverse party.

Bryce does not dispute that the statements in the Johnson–Gomez tape were material, that the declarants were unable to testify, or that the government complied with the Rule's notice requirement. The resolution of this argument is therefore linked most importantly to an evaluation of trustworthiness or reliability.

Under the hearsay rules, courts must evaluate the totality of the circumstances to determine whether a statement contains particular guarantees of trustworthiness that make the declaration especially worthy of belief. The Court listed several factors to consider in determining reliability including 1) the spontaneity of the statement; 2) the consistency of the statement; 3) the lack of motive to fabricate; 4) the reason the declarant will not testify; and 5) the voluntariness of the statement.

The statements at issue in the Johnson–Gomez tape have a high degree of trustworthiness. As we noted in *United States v. Matthews* (15th Cir. 1994):

> [O]rdinarily, a confession of an accomplice resulting from formal police interrogation cannot be introduced as evidence of the guilt of an accused, absent some circumstance indicating authorization or adoption. On the other hand, if the statement is made to a person whom the declarant believes is an ally rather than a law enforcement official, and if the circumstances surrounding the portion of the statement that inculpates the defendant provide no reason to suspect that that inculpatory portion is any less trustworthy than the part of the statement that directly incriminates the declarant, the trustworthiness of the portion that inculpates the defendant may well be sufficiently established that its admission does not violate the hearsay rule.

Several factors prove particularly relevant in this case: (i) the statements were obtained via a covert wiretap of which neither Johnson nor Gomez was aware; (ii) the statements were made during the same time period that Johnson was conversing with Bryce; (iii) Johnson's statements implicated both himself and Bryce as participants in a narcotics conspiracy; and (iv) Gomez was Johnson's colleague in the narcotics trade. Based on these factors, there is little reason to believe that Johnson and Gomez had any motive to lie, or were lying, during this telephone conversation. Accordingly, the district court's decision to admit the Johnson–Gomez tape was proper under Rule 807.

Affirmed.

PT-B: SELECTED ANSWER 1

MEMORANDUM

TO: Penny Andrews

FROM: Applicant

RE: Rock v. Davis and Bond

DATE: February 27, 2014

The General Rule Regarding Hearsay

Under Rule 801 of the Federal Rules of Evidence (FRE), a statement made by a declarant at any other time besides while testifying at the current trial may not be admitted as evidence to prove the truth of the matter asserted in the statement unless a federal statute, the FRE, or other rules prescribed by the Supreme Court otherwise provide. We seek to introduce the trial transcript, voice mail message transcript, and transcript of the telephone conversation between Mr. Watts and Ms. Hill for the truth of the statements asserted therein. That is, we seek to admit them as evidence that Mr. Watts did not, in fact, see Mr. Rock shoot anybody and that his contrary assertions during the police investigation and to the grand jury were coerced by Officers Davis and Bond. Therefore, in order for the evidence to be admissible, it must fall within an exception to the hearsay rules. There are three relevant hearsay exceptions that might apply to the transcripts at issue here: the exception for former testimony of an unavailable declarant, the exception for a statement against interest of an unavailable declarant, and the residual exception. I will address each in turn.

Former Testimony Exception

Under FRE 804, when a declarant is unavailable, a declarant's former testimony, given as a witness at a trial, hearing, or lawful deposition, is admissible if it is now offered against a party — or in a civil case like ours, a predecessor in interest — who had an opportunity and similar motive to develop the testimony. Thus, in order to offer hearsay under this rule a party must show that (1) the declarant is unavailable; (2) the declarant made the statements at issue when he was a witness at a trial, hearing, or lawful deposition; (3) the evidence is being offered against the same party or a predecessor in interest who (4) had an opportunity and (5) similar motive to develop the testimony.

Unavailability

Rule 804 provides that that former testimony exception applies to a witness who is unavailable because he has died. Mr. Watts died in a liquor store robbery, and therefore is unavailable within the meaning of the Rule.

Statements at Issue Were Made While a Witness

The statements of Mr. Watts at Mr. Rock's trial were made while a witness during a trial. Therefore, if they meet the other criteria for admissibility under this exception, they are admissible thereunder. The statements made on Ms. Hill's voicemail, however, as well as those Mr. Watts made in conversation with Ms. Hill, were not trial, hearing, or deposition testimony. Therefore, they cannot be admitted under the exception for former testimony.

Same Party or Predecessor in Interest

As noted above, Rule 804 provides that to be admissible under this exception, the former testimony must be offered against the same party or a predecessor in interest who had a prior opportunity and motive to develop it. Defense counsel will likely argue that the prosecutor in Mr. Rock's criminal trial was not a predecessor in interest to the police defendants in the present action. In doing so, defendants will probably rely on the Fifteenth Circuit's opinion in Hannah v. City of Overland. Similar to Mr. Rock's case, the plaintiff in that case after being unsuccessfully criminally prosecuted brought a civil action against the City and the police for conduct related to his arrest and detention. He sought to introduce in his civil case, under the former testimony exception, a deposition of a declarant who had died. The deposition was taken by the plaintiff's criminal defense counsel in advance of his criminal trial. The prosecutor was present at the deposition, but no representatives of the police officers, who were defendants in the civil case, were present. In deciding that the deposition was inadmissible, the Fifteenth Circuit assumed without deciding that the prosecutor was a predecessor in interest of the civil defendants, but noted that that proposition was "by no means clear." (*Hannah* 7). Defendants will likely attempt to capitalize on the doubt created by the Fifteenth Circuit, and argue that the prosecutor in Mr. Rock's trial was not a predecessor in interest to Detectives Davis and Bond.

There are several arguments with which this contention can be countered. First and most importantly, the Fifteenth Circuit decided Hannah on other grounds. It explicitly did not decide the question of whether a prosecutor can be considered a predecessor in interest of civil defendant police officers. Therefore, it is dicta that offers little guidance. Furthermore, although the Circuit did state that the issue was unclear, it also assumed that the prosecutor was, in fact, a predecessor in interest. In addition, the circumstances of this case suggest that the prosecutor was a predecessor in interest of the civil defendants here, even if that is not always the case. The court of appeals in *Hannah* noted that there were no representatives of the defendants in that case present when the deposition testimony at issue was offered. That is not the case here. Ms. Hill told you in your interview with her that the prosecutor gave the detectives dirty looks when Mr. Watts recanted, indicating that the detectives were present in the courtroom. In addition, Ms. Hill speculated that the prosecutor did not attempt to rehabilitate Mr. Watts because he was worried about subjecting the city to civil liability. If this is true — a question you might seek to explore further before — then the prosecutor was considering civil liability in his conduct — precisely the liability at issue here. As the detectives' employer, the city's liability will likely stem from that of the detectives.

In sum, I think there is a reasonable argument that despite the dicta in Hannah, the district attorney in this case can be considered a predecessor in interest of the detectives. However, this argument may be a difficult one.

Opportunity to Develop Testimony

Even if the district attorney can be considered the detectives' successor in interest, in order for the trial transcript to be admissible as former testimony, he must have had an opportunity to develop Mr. Watts' testimony through direct, cross-examination, or redirect examination. Here, although the district attorney made no effort to rehabilitate Mr. Watts, he certainly had the opportunity to do so. Mr. Watts retracted his testimony on direct examination, which the prosecutor could have continued had he wished to do so. In fact, Ms. Hill stated that the court prompted the district attorney and still he did not develop Mr. Watts' testimony further. The trial testimony thus satisfies this component of the exception.

Motive to Develop Testimony

In order for Mr. Watts' trial testimony to be admitted, you will have to demonstrate that the district attorney had a similar motive to develop the testimony that the detective defendants have now.

Defense counsel will likely argue, relying on *Hannah*, that the district attorney did not have a similar motive as the detective defendants in Mr. Rock's case. In *Hannah*, the court of appeals held that the deposition testimony at issue could not be admitted under the former testimony exception because the prosecutor had no significant motive, let alone a similar motive, to develop the testimony of the declarant. The circumstances in *Hannah*, however, were quite different than those during Mr. Rock's criminal trial. In *Hannah*, the prosecution's case relied in large part on the testimony of one witness. The *Hannah* plaintiff sought to admit deposition testimony of a *different* witness, stating that his initial statements were coerced by the police. But, because the prosecution was relying almost entirely on another witness, these statements were "of little, if any, concern to the State at" the time. (*Hannah 7*). That is, the prosecutor in that case had little, if any motive, to cross-examine that witness because his statements were largely irrelevant to the case — therefore, whether they were coerced did not matter.

Here, in contrast, Mr. Watts was the sole witness against Mr. Rock. Therefore, once Mr. Watts recanted, the success of Mr. Rock's prosecution hinged entirely on whether Mr. Watts was being truthful about his recantation and the coercion by the police. Therefore, the district attorney had a strong motive to try to rehabilitate his testimony, if he believed he could do so. That he did not do so is much more likely evidence that he believed Mr. Watts that his testimony was, in fact, coerced, and not that he lacked motive to develop Mr. Watts' testimony. Furthermore, the reason he did not develop Mr. Watts' testimony may, as noted, have been a fear of civil liability — that is, knowledge that Mr. Watts testimony was likely coerced and a fear of a civil suit, like this one, based on such coercion. Whether the development of Mr. Watts' testimony would lead to civil liability is the same consideration the counsel for the detectives in Mr. Rock's civil suit would likely rely on to determine whether to further question Mr. Watts. However, whether the district was in fact considering civil liability is mere supposition. To strongly support an argument that the district attorney had a sufficiently similar motive, more evidence of this consideration would likely be needed.

The Fifteenth Circuit, in *Hannah*, stated that to assess similarity of motive, a court should determine whether "the party resisting the offered testimony" previously had "an interest of substantially similar intensity to prove (or disprove) the same side of a substantially similar issue." (*Hannah 6*). The court explained that the "nature of the two proceedings — both what is at stake and the applicable burden of proof" as well as, but to a lesser extent, the cross-examination at the first proceeding "will be relevant though not conclusive." (*Id.*) Here, the two proceedings at issue had different stakes, but as noted you could argue that the district attorney was considering civil liability as well, and therefore the nature of the proceedings is not as different as it may seem. The question of the burden of proof, however, may be trickier. Defense counsel will likely argue that the district attorney did not further develop Mr. Watts' testimony because he believed that even with rehabilitation, he could not overcome the burden of proof required to convict Mr. Rock. The burden of proof in Mr. Rock's civil case is likely to be much lower than that of the defense attorney. With respect to the cross-examination factors, the district attorney did not cross-examine Mr. Rock at all, and forewent any opportunity to develop his testimony. Defense counsel will likely argue that based on these factors, even if the district attorney had a similar motive to disprove Mr. Watts' testimony, his interest was not of a substantially similar intensity to that of the defendant detectives. The district attorney, defense counsel may argue, may have had an interest not only in convicting Mr. Rock but also in avoiding civil liability. But he may have thought once Mr. Watts recanted, conviction was impossible given the burden of proof. In addition, because, unlike the detective defendants, he would not be the one held civilly liable, his interest in avoiding civil liability would not be as strong as that of the detectives. Although there is a reasonable argument that the district attorney's interest in disproving Mr. Watts' recantation is substantially similar to the interest of the defendant detectives, the argument that that interest is of substantially similar intensity to that of the detectives is weaker.

In conclusion, given the difficulty of demonstrating a substantially similar interest of a substantially similar intensity, and because only trial testimony can be admitted under this exception, other exceptions provide better options for the admissibility of the transcripts.

Statement Against Interest Exception

FRE Rule 804(b) provides that where a declarant is unavailable, the declarant's hearsay statement may be admissible if (1) it is "so contrary to the declarant's" pecuniary or penal interests that a reasonable person would not have made the statement unless it was true; and (2) if it is offered in a criminal case as a statement that "tends to expose the declarant to criminal liability," it must be "supported by corroborating circumstances that clearly indicate its trustworthiness." As noted above, because Mr. Watts is dead, he is considered unavailable within the meaning of the FRE.

Contrary to Declarant's Pecuniary or Penal Interest

Mr. Watts' statements in each of the transcripts you seek to admit would likely be considered contrary to his penal interest. The Fifteenth Circuit has explained that "[a] reasonable person would know that admitting to give false testimony would subject the person to criminal liability for perjury." (Cabrera 10). Here, Mr. Watts testified in front of the grand jury that he had seen Mr. Rock committing the shooting. Mr. Watts' recantation at trial, his statements on Ms. Hill's voicemail that his previous statements and testimony inculpating Mr. Rock were "not true," and his similar statements in his telephone conversation with Ms. Hill all directly contradict Mr. Watts' testimony under oath at the grand jury proceeding. Indeed, Mr. Watts' statements in the transcript admit that he lied under oath. As noted by the Fifteenth Circuit, such statements would subject him to criminal liability such that a reasonable person would not have made them if they were not true. In considering precisely the same circumstances — a witness who gave inculpatory testimony under oath against a defendant and then later stated that her testimony was untrue and coerced — the Fifteenth Circuit in United States v. Cabrera stated that the later statements were clearly against the declarant's penal interest as required to fulfill the statement against interest exception. It is important to note that the Fifteenth Circuit decided Cabrera on other grounds. However, the Circuit fully explained its reasoning for characterizing as against penal interest statements in which a declarant admits previous testimony was untrue. In addition, the Circuit was definitive in its statement. Therefore, it is useful support for the argument that Watts' statements in all three of the transcripts you seek to admit are against penal interest. In any event, there should be little difficulty demonstrating that Watts' statements were against penal interest.

Corroborating Evidence, if Offered in a Criminal Case

As noted above Rule 804(b) provides that, "if it is offered in a criminal case," a statement against the declarant's penal interest and tending to exculpate the accused is only admissible if there are corroborating circumstances that indicate the truthfulness of the statement. (FRE Rule 804(b)(3)(B) (emphasis added)). Defense counsel may argue that there is insufficient corroborating circumstances to indicate the truthfulness of Watts' statements at trial or in the post-trial voicemail and phone conversation. But Rule 804(b) explicitly states that such corroborating circumstances are required only if the hearsay statement is being offered in a criminal case. Mr. Rock's case is civil. Therefore, under the language of the Rule, the transcripts should be admissible in Mr. Rock's case against the detectives regardless of whether there are corroborating circumstances that indicate the truthfulness of the statements.

Residual Exception

Rule 807 of the FRE provides an exception to hearsay statements not otherwise admissible under the FRE. That rule provides that a hearsay statement is admissible if: (1) the statement has equivalent circumstantial guarantees of trustworthiness; (2) it is offered as evidence of a material fact; (3) it is more probative on the point for which it is offered than any other evidence that the proponent can obtain through reasonable efforts; and (4) admitting it will best serve the purposes of these rules and the interests of justice.

The transcripts at issue likely satisfy the second and third prongs of this exception. If the police coerced Mr. Watts' statements at their interview and in front of the grand jury, then they knew they did not have probable cause to arrest and detain him. As Mr. Rock is claiming false arrest and imprisonment (among other things), this is central to his case. In addition, the only other evidence Mr. Rock can likely obtain on this point is the detectives' testimony, and that testimony is likely to be self-serving. Mr. Watts' statements, on the other hand, could subject him to criminal liability for perjury.

Therefore, Mr. Watts' statements in the transcript are more probative on the point than any other testimony Mr. Rock can likely obtain through reasonable efforts.

You may have difficulty, however, satisfying the requirement that there be circumstantial guarantees of trustworthiness. The Fifteenth Circuit has approved a district court opinion which relied on several factors in assessing trustworthiness. Those factors include the spontaneity of the statement; the consistency of the statement; the lack of motive to fabricate; the reason the declarant is unavailable; and the voluntariness of the statement. Here, Watts' statement appears to be spontaneous and voluntary. Watts initiated the phone call to Mr. Rock's counsel, and there is no indication he was coerced into doing so — indeed, he specifically denied such coercion. In addition, his unavailability does not cast suspicion on his testimony; he cannot testify because of his death. These factors weigh in favor of admitting the statement. However, it appears that Watts was friends with Mr. Rock. This indicates a possible motive to fabricate. However, given that his recantation subjected him to criminal liability, any motive to fabricate based on his friendship is likely to be overcome by the motive not to make statements against penal interest unless truthful. The most difficult problem you face in demonstrating that there are circumstantial guarantees of trustworthiness, however, is that some of the details of Mr. Watts' story changed as he recounted it. First, of course, is the problem that he initially testified at the grand jury (and stated during the police investigation) that Mr. Rock committed the shooting. Perhaps more importantly, even once he recanted he kept changing the reason he felt coerced: At trial he stated that the pressure he felt from the police related somehow to his mom's house, but on the voicemail message to Ms. Hill he stated that the pressure was because the police were trying to blame him, and in his phone conversation with Ms. Hill, he stated that the detective slapped him. Defense counsel will likely argue that this changing story is evidence that Mr. Watts' statements are untrustworthy. You could argue that his statements were different, but not inconsistent — detectives could have threatened his mom's house, blamed him, and hit him. It is unlikely however that a truthful declarant would give different reasons for different statements. You could also argue that these matters are collateral — Mr. Watts' basic statement that the police coerced him into testifying falsely has remained unchanged throughout. This may, however, be a difficult argument.

Furthermore, in addition to demonstrating that there are circumstantial guarantees of trustworthiness, to admit Watts' statements, you'd need also demonstrate that there would be a risk of miscarriage of justice if the statements are not admitted. Although these statements are more important to Watts' civil case than statements the Fifteenth Circuit has previously excluded (see *Hannah*), the failure to impose civil liability is less of a miscarriage of justice than a wrongful conviction. Therefore, though I think you can successfully argue that admission of the transcripts are in the interest of justice, the interest is not as strong as if it were a criminal case.

The Fifteenth Circuit has held that the requirements of this hearsay exception is to be "construed narrowly." (*Hannah*) Because of the inconsistency of Mr. Watts' statements, I think you will have trouble admitting them under the exception if it is narrowly construed.

Conclusion

As explained above, the hearsay exception for statements against interest is likely to be the most successful argument for admission of all the transcripts.

PT-B: SELECTED ANSWER 2

To: Penny Andrews
From: Applicant
Date: Feb 27, 2014

Re: Rock v. Davis and Bond, Objective Memorandum on Defendants' Motion in Limine

Summary

We represent Plaintiff Gerald Rock (Rock) in his civil suit against Defendants Richard Davis (Davis) and Thomas Bond (Bond) for false arrest and imprisonment and malicious prosecution. A large portion of our evidence relates to testimony from a witness, Joe Watts (Watts), in Rock's prior criminal case for a shooting. In particular, Watts initially implicated Rock as the shooter and identified Rock in a grand jury proceeding, but then recanted his statement in a phone call to the defense attorney as well as in court.

Defendants have denied each of our claims, asserted affirmative defenses, and moved *in limine* to exclude, as hearsay, evidence of all transcripts or testimony concerning the prior testimony of Watts. The hearing is set for March 6, 2014 at 9:00 a.m.

Per your request, this objective memorandum identifies and discusses each of defendants' likely assertions for the motion *in limine,* our possible counter arguments, and the likely result. Specifically, defendants will argue that Watts' statements: (I) are hearsay, (II) do not qualify under Fed R. Evid. 804(b)(1) as a former testimony exception, (III) do not qualify under Fed. R. Evid. 804(b)(3) as a statement against interest, and (IV) do not qualify under Fed. R. Evid. 807(a)'s residual exception. Each of these arguments is discussed in turn.

Analysis

I.   Whether Rock's Statements Are Hearsay

a. Watts' Testimony

Defendants have moved *in limine* to exclude Watts' testimony as hearsay. In particular, Watts' prior testimony includes:

--Testimony from the trial transcript in the case of State of Columbia v. Rock. For example, in response to the DA's question, "Are you now telling us you did not see the defendant shoot the victim?" Watts replies, "Yes." Then when asked why Watts told the police that he saw Rock shoot the victim, Watts responds, "Because I was forced under pressure, sir."

--Trial transcript testimony, Defense Exhibit 1 (Exhibit 1), which is a transcript of the voice mail message left by Watts to Defense Attorney Didi Hill on September 9, 2011. For example, Watts says he "fingered Gerry for the shooting" at both his initial discussion with the police and in his grand jury testimony because the police "were trying to blame [him]" and pressured him.

--Trial transcript testimony, Defense Exhibit 2 (Exhibit 2), which is a transcript of a telephone conversation between Watts and Defense Attorney Hill on September 9, 2011. For example, the transcript says Watts never saw Gerald shoot towards the courthouse. Watts also says the detective told him to say something and said, "You better start talking . . ." and then slapped him.

b. Rule Against Hearsay

Pursuant to Fed. R. Evid. 801, hearsay is a (1) statement by a declarant, other than a statement made while testifying at the current trial or hearing, that is (2) offered to prove the truth of the matter asserted in the statement. Unless otherwise provided for in a federal statute, the rules, or other Supreme Court rules, hearsay is not admissible.

(1) Statement made by a declarant other than at trial

Here, the statements are made by Watts, a person declarant, not while he is testifying in the current case.

(2) Statement offered to prove the truth of the matter asserted

Here, the statements would be offered to show that Rock did not shoot the victim and that Davis and Bond were coercing Watts to implicate Rock. This will support our claim that Rock was falsely arrested and imprisoned, that Defendants acted maliciously and willfully, and that Rock was maliciously prosecuted by Defendants. This will also negate Defendants' affirmative defenses that there was probable cause for the arrest, that Rock's injuries stemmed from his own culpable conduct, and that Defendants acted reasonably and under qualified immunity.

Thus, the testimony is hearsay and is inadmissible unless otherwise provided for in a federal rule (assuming no supreme court rules or statutes apply). Here, it is possible that the statements fall under exceptions for former testimony, statements against interest, or residual.

II. Whether Rock's Statements Fall Under the Former Testimony Exception

a. Unavailable

The former testimony exception only applies if the declarant cannot be present or testify at trial or hearing due to, *inter alia*, death. Here, Watts died last week and thus is unavailable to testify.

b. Former Testimony

Pursuant to Fed. R. Evid. 804(b)(1), hearsay is admissible under the former testimony exception if it (1) was given as a witness at a trial, hearing, or lawful deposition, whether given during the current proceeding or a different one, and (2) is now offered against a party who had -- or, in a civil case, whose predecessor in interest had -- an opportunity and similar motive to develop it by direct, cross, or redirect examination.

(1)   Trial, hearing, or lawful deposition

Here, under the first prong of the test, the direct examination of Watts was testimony at a prior hearing. Thus, those statements satisfy the first element of the prior testimony exception. However, Exhibit 1 was a voice mail message outside of a trial, hearing, deposition or similar proceeding. Likewise, Exhibit 2 is a telephone conversation outside of a trial or hearing. Thus, the exhibits do not satisfy the former hearsay exception.

(2)   Against a party who had an opportunity and similar motive to develop the testimony

Opportunity:

The second prong of the former testimony exception requires both an opportunity and a similar motive to develop testimony. For example, in *Hannah*, the Fifteenth Circuit affirmed denial of deposition testimony in a section 1983 suit against the city and police force when the deposition stated that the witness implicated the plaintiff (and former arrestee) because he was "pressured" and "threatened' by the police to cooperate. The court noted that, although the prosecutor's office represented the State at the depositions, there were no representatives for the defendants. Nonetheless, the court assumed, arguendo, that the prosecutor was the police personnel's "predecessor in interest" and that the prosecutor had an "opportunity" to develop the testimony.

Here, there is no evidence that Davis' or Bond's attorneys were present for Watts' trial proceedings. Rather, the DA gave the direct examination of Watts and attorney Hill gave the cross-examination. Thus, like Hannah, we would need to argue that the DA was a predecessor in interest for Davis and Bond. While the Hannah court noted the proposition was unclear, it went forward with this assumption. If the court does the same thing as in Hannah, we would be able to show that the DA had an opportunity to develop the testimony because the DA gave the direct examination and could have rebutted Hill's line of questioning. Thus, this part of the test is satisfied.

Motive:

Similar motive requires a substantially similar intensity to prove (or disprove) the same side of a substantially similar issue. Hannah. The nature of the two proceedings — both what is at stake and the applicable burden of proof — and, to a lesser extent, the cross-examination at the prior proceeding — both what was undertaken and what was available but forgone — are relevant, although not conclusive. In Hannah, the court found the prosecutor did not have a "similar motive" to develop the testimony because the testimony was not of great importance to the case. For instance, the court highlighted the fact that the plaintiff had already been arrested and indicted by a grand jury and that the State's case rested largely upon testimony of another witness, Beede. In fact, Beede testified that the plaintiff had admitted guilt to him, and the witness's deposition testimony merely corroborated Beede's statements. Thus, the statements that the witness had been "threatened" and "pressured" were of little concern to the State, and thus the State did not have a significant or "similar" motive to develop the testimony.

Here, Defendants will argue that, like Hannah, the DA did not have the same interests in developing the testimony. Defendants will likely argue that the DA's motives are not similar, potentially because the DA's time and resources are limited; whereas, Defendants' livelihoods and reputations are at stake. Therefore, Defendants may have had a stronger motive to develop Watts' testimony. In fact, attorney Hill noted that Defendants and the DA exchanged "a lot of dirty looks" when the DA did not rehabilitate Watts after Watts said that he had lied. Therefore, Defendants will argue that the statements regarding threats or pressure to implicate a certain person should be inadmissible hearsay, as in Hannah.

However, our case is distinguishable from *Hannah* on several facts. Here, Rock was arrested after (and likely because of) Watts' identification. Prior to that identification, Defendants only had an anonymous 911 call about Watts at the scene of the crime. Further, Watts identified Rock as the shooter at the grand jury proceedings. Thus, unlike Hannah, Rock's arrest and indictment rest largely on, or potentially solely on, Watts' testimony. By contrast, *Hannah* involved evidence from another witness and a prior, independent arrest and indictment.

Moreover, the court in Hannah highlighted that the State did not have a substantial motive to develop the deposition testimony about police misconduct because there was other substantial evidence implicating the accused. Here, however, the DA did not have any other evidence after Watts' trial testimony; and the DA's only witness was Watts. Without anything further, the court granted Hill's motion for a directed verdict. Thus, the DA had a significant motive to develop Watts' testimony because the case rested upon it.

Finally, Fed. R. Evid. 804(b)(1) does not require the same motive, but only similar motive. Given this language, as well as the comparisons with Hannah, a court will likely conclude that this element is satisfied. The DA's motive was to rehabilitate Watts with earlier testimony as its only witness, and Defendants' motive would have been to rehabilitate Watts because Watts' two prior identifications support their defense in the current case.

Thus, the court will likely not admit Exhibit 1 or 2 under the former testimony exception because the voicemail and telephone conversation were not at prior trials proceedings or hearings. However, if the court finds the DA to be a predecessor in interest to Defendants, then the court will likely admit the trial transcript under the former testimony proceeding given the importance of Watts' earlier testimony and the DA's corresponding similar motive to develop that testimony.

III. Whether Rock's Statements Fall Under the Statement Against Interest Exception

a. Unavailable

The statement against interest exception applies if the declarant is unavailable. As noted above, Watts is unavailable due to death.

b. Statement Against Interest

Pursuant to Fed. R. Evid. 804(b)(3), hearsay is admissible under the statement against interest exception if (1) a reasonable person in the declarant's position would have made the statement only if the person believed it to be true because, when made, it was so contrary to the declarant's proprietary or pecuniary interest or had so great a tendency to invalidate the declarant's claim against someone else or to expose the declarant to civil or criminal liability, and (2) is supported by corroborating circumstances that clearly indicate its trustworthiness, if it is offered in a criminal case as one that tends to expose the declarant to criminal liability.

1.   Statement against civil or criminal liability so that a reasonable person would not have made the statement unless believing it to be true

In *Cabrera*, the Fifteenth Circuit found that a statement that a witness did not testify truthfully at trial was against penal interest because it amounted to a "squarely self-inculpatory confession." In other words, a reasonable person would not have made the statement unless believing it to be truth because she would know that admitting to giving false testimony would subject the person to criminal liability for perjury, especially absent any grant of immunity. Specifically, in that case, a witness testified at trial that a belt used in a murder likely belonged to the defendant. Then several months later, after the trial, the witness sought to recant her testimony on the grounds that she was coerced into giving perjured testimony.

Applying *Cabrera,* the determination of whether a statement is against penal interest (i.e., because it will subject the speaker to criminal liability), depends on whether the defendant would be subject to perjury for making false statements. Perjury generally requires a false statement of material fact made under oath. Thus, Watts' statements should be divided up between his grand jury statements, which were presumably under oath, and his other statements.

Statement leading to arrest:

After Davis went to pick up Watts, Watts identified Rock as one of the shooters. Rock was then arrested. These statements were likely not under oath. Thus, these statements to Davis likely do not fall under this application of the statement against hearsay exception. Thus, the trial transcript portions which discuss the statements made to the police up to the point of the grand jury proceeding are not admissible under this rule. This includes the trial transcript portions where Watts said he lied and said that the shooter was Rock and that he said that because he was forced under pressure and was lying.

However, these statements could be statements against penal interest if they were incorporated into Watts' statements to the grand jury (see below).

Statement at grand jury proceeding:

Watts also gave statements in the grand jury proceedings, and those statements likely were under oath. Thus, those statements will likely fall under the statement against interest exception. For example, in Exhibit 1, Watts says he just testified at the grand jury and got the same pressure and that he lied again, telling them Rock did the shooting. If Watts' statements at the grand jury proceeding were under oath, then his statements in Exhibit 1 would be against his penal interest because he would be subject to perjury for lying in the grand jury proceeding. Thus, this exception likely applies to these statements.

Statements about post-grand jury proceedings:

In Exhibit 2, Watts talks about discussions with the detective and that he said, "Oh, I know what happened" and "You better start talking." Those statements were not under oath, and likely do not fall under the statement against interest exception.

Other types of interests:

We could also argue that Watts' statements were made against another type of interest, other than a penal interest. However, Watts did not appear to be at risk for any other type of civil or proprietary liability for making his statements regarding pressure from Defendants to implicate Rock. Thus, this argument will likely fail.

2. *Corroborating circumstances*

In *Cabrera,* the court did not admit hearsay under the statement against interest exception because it found lack of corroborating circumstances. In particular, it noted that the recanting statement was made more than six months after the trial testimony; this large temporal gap and lack of spontaneity did not support the admissibility of the statement.

Here, Defendants may argue that there are no corroborating circumstances because nothing else seems to support Watts' statements that he was pressured into implicating Rock. However, under the language of Fed. R. Evid. 804(b)(3), the corroborating circumstances requirement only comes into play if the statement is made in a criminal case and tends to expose the declarant to criminal liability. For example, in Cabrera, the case was United States v. Cabrera, a criminal case seeking a new trial. Here, by contrast, Rock's lawsuit against Defendants is a civil suit for general, special, and punitive damages. Thus, corroborating circumstances are not required.

If they were required, however, our case is also distinguishable from Cabrera because that case involved a recanting statement more than six months after trial testimony. Here, however, Watts wanted to recant his statements during a trial proceeding. Further, the arrest occurred on August 29, 2011; Watts left the voicemail and spoke with attorney Hill (Exhibits 1 and 2) on September 9, 2011. Thus, the statements are likely corroborated by their proximity in time and apparent spontaneity. Cabrera.

IV. Whether Rock's Statements Fall Under the Residual Exception

Pursuant to Fed. R. Evid. 807, hearsay is not excluded under the residual exception if (1) the statement has circumstantial guarantees of trustworthiness, (2) it is offered as evidence of a material fact, (3) it is more probative on the point for which it is offered than any other evidence the proponent can obtain through reasonable efforts, and (4) admitting it will serve the purposes of the rules and the interests of justice. Additionally, (5) the proponent must give the adverse party reasonable notice of the intent to offer the statement before trial or hearing.

a. Residual Exception

The residual

1. *Circumstantial guarantees of trustworthiness*

Circumstantial guarantees of trustworthiness are similar to the corroborating circumstances requirement for the statement against interest exception. See Cabrera (denying admission under the residual exception for the same reasons that it denied it under the statement against interest exception). More specifically, in determining trustworthiness or reliability, the court may consider several factors, including (1) the spontaneity of the statement, (2) the consistency of the statement, (3) the lack of motive to fabricate, (4) the reason the declarant will not testify, and (5) the voluntariness of the statement.

Spontaneity:

Here, Watts' statements in Exhibit 1 and 2 were spontaneous and made upon his own accord. By contrast, Defendants would argue that the statements in the trial proceeding were prompted by the DA. Thus, the former statements are more spontaneous and more likely to be admissible under this exception than the latter statements. Also, as noted above, this case is distinguishable from *Cabrera*, in which the declarant waited six months to recant her statement. Here, Watts wanted to recant his statement no more than one month after he said he had lied.

Consistency:

Here, there is consistency between the statements in Exhibit 1, Exhibit 2, and the trial transcript. Specifically, Exhibit 1 says that Watts said Rock did the shooting but that he lied; the police were trying to blame him, and they pressured him at the time of the arrest and prior to the grand jury proceeding. Similarly, Exhibit 2 says he never saw Rock at the courthouse, did not see him shoot; he also said that the detectives were threatening him. In the trial transcript, Rock likewise testifies that he did not see Rock shoot the victim and that he lied before because he was forced into his testimony under pressure. Further, when asked how the police were questioning him, Watts says (before being cut off), that the police said his mom's house could get . . ."

Thus, there is consistency in the statements that Watts did see Rock shoot the victim and that he made previous statements because of police pressure. Thus, this element sides with inclusion of the statements.

Lack of motive to lie:

In *Matthews*, the court noted that a confession of an accomplice from a police interrogation cannot ordinarily be introduced as evidence of guilt of an accused. However, if a statement is made to a person who is viewed as an ally, rather than a law enforcement official, and if the circumstances surrounding the portion that inculpates the defendant provide no reason to suspect that the inculpatory portion is any less trustworthy than the part that directly incriminates the declarant, then trustworthiness may be sufficiently established.

For example, in *Bryce*, the Fifteenth Circuit admitted hearsay statements from a phone call between two supposed co-conspirators. In doing so, it noted several "particularly relevant" facts, including the fact that the statements were made by a covert wiretap of which neither speaker was aware, the statements were made during the same time period as other admitted statements, the statements implicated the speaker and the defendant, and the speaker and defendant were colleagues. Accordingly, the court found there was little reason for either party to have the motive to lie.

Here, Defendants will likely argue that the trial transcript testimony was not voluntary because it was made in court after DA questioning; thus, this would fall under the general rule not allowing confessions in response to police interrogation. Defendants will likely win this argument.

However, we have a strong response that Exhibits 1 and 2 were voluntary and not made in response to police interrogation or anything similar. In fact, Exhibit 1 includes Watts' completely voluntary voice mail left to attorney Hill; there was no prompting from Hill or the government. Further, Watts may have viewed Hill as an "ally" because she was representing Rock against the government, and Watts wanted to protect Rock and speak out against the government. While Hill was not the same type of ally as the drug co-conspirator in Bryce (as Defendants might point out), Hill is likely viewed more as an ally than an adversarial police. Also, like *Bryce*, Watts likely did not know his telephone conversation was recorded; while he knew the voice mail in Exhibit 1 was recorded, he probably did not know that either Exhibit 1 or 2 would be used in court when he made the statements. Additionally, like Bryce, Watts' statements implicated himself as well as Defendants because Watts could be later tried for perjury. Thus, the Exhibits 1 and 2 demonstrate no motive to lie, and thus have circumstantial guarantees of trustworthiness.

Reason declarant will not testify:

Here, Watts will not testify due to his death; thus, this element favors inclusion of the testimony.

Voluntariness:

As analyzed in the section above for motive to lie, the statements made in the trial proceeding were not voluntary because they were in response to DA questioning; however, the Exhibit 1 and 2 statements were voluntarily made.

2.   *Material fact*

The statements are material facts concerning whether Defendants coerced Watts into lying and are therefore liable for improper arrest, imprisonment, and malicious prosecutions.

3.   *More probative than other evidence*

Watts' statements are more probative than other evidence. No other similar evidence is indicated, and Watts can no longer be retained because he is dead.

4.   Interests of justice

The residual exception is "construed narrowly" so that it does not swallow the hearsay rule. Cabrera. For example, excluding evidence would not pose a great risk of miscarriage of justice if it was weak and related to only one small link among several implicating factors. Id. (finding statement that witness lied at a trial six months prior not admissible under the residual exception because there were other implicating factors, including other physical evidence and expert testimony connecting defendant to the scene of the crime).

b. Notice

If the statements are to be used, we would need to give the proper notice to Defendants.

Thus, Exhibits 1 and 2 likely fall under the residual exception because they are material and evidence circumstantial guarantees of trustworthiness.

Conclusion

For the aforementioned reasons, we have strong arguments in reply to Defendants' motion *in limine* to exclude Watts' statements as hearsay. Specifically, the trial testimony likely falls under the former testimony and statement against interest exceptions. The statements in Exhibit 1 and 2 may be admissible under the residual exception if the court finds that in the interests.